An Analysis of

Philippe Ariès's

Centuries of Childhood
A Social History of Family Life

Eva-Marie Prag
with
Joseph Tendler

Published by Macat International Ltd
24:13 Coda Centre, 189 Munster Road, London SW6 6AW.

Distributed exclusively by Routledge
2 Park Square, Milton Park, Abingdon, Oxon OX14 4RN
711 Third Avenue, New York, NY 10017, USA

Routledge is an imprint of the Taylor & Francis Group, an informa business

www.macat.com
info@macat.com

Cataloguing in Publication Data
A catalogue record for this book is available from the British Library.
Library of Congress Cataloguing-in-Publication Data is available upon request.
Cover illustration: Kim Thompson

ISBN 978-1-912302-42-0 (hardback)
ISBN 978-1-912128-81-5 (paperback)
ISBN 978-1-912281-30-5 (e-book)

Notice
The information in this book is designed to orientate readers of the work under analysis,
to elucidate and contextualise its key ideas and themes, and to aid in the development
of critical thinking skills. It is not meant to be used, nor should it be used, as a
substitute for original thinking or in place of original writing or research. References and
notes are provided for informational purposes and their presence does not constitute
endorsement of the information or opinions therein. This book is presented solely for
educational purposes. It is sold on the understanding that the publisher is not engaged
to provide any scholarly advice. The publisher has made every effort to ensure that
this book is accurate and up-to-date, but makes no warranties or representations with
regard to the completeness or reliability of the information it contains. The information
and the opinions provided herein are not guaranteed or warranted to produce particular
results and may not be suitable for students of every ability. The publisher shall not be
liable for any loss, damage or disruption arising from any errors or omissions, or from
the use of this book, including, but not limited to, special, incidental, consequential or
other damages caused, or alleged to have been caused, directly or indirectly, by the
information contained within.

CONTENTS

THE MACAT LIBRARY

The Macat Library is a series of unique academic explorations of seminal works in the humanities and social sciences – books and papers that have had a significant and widely recognised impact on their disciplines. It has been created to serve as much more than just a summary of what lies between the covers of a great book. It illuminates and explores the influences on, ideas of, and impact of that book. Our goal is to offer a learning resource that encourages critical thinking and fosters a better, deeper understanding of important ideas.

Each publication is divided into three Sections: Influences, Ideas, and Impact. Each Section has four Modules. These explore every important facet of the work, and the responses to it.

This Section-Module structure makes a Macat Library book easy to use, but it has another important feature. Because each Macat book is written to the same format, it is possible (and encouraged!) to cross-reference multiple Macat books along the same lines of inquiry or research. This allows the reader to open up interesting interdisciplinary pathways.

To further aid your reading, lists of glossary terms and people mentioned are included at the end of this book (these are indicated by an asterisk [*] throughout) – as well as a list of works cited.

Macat has worked with the University of Cambridge to identify the elements of critical thinking and understand the ways in which six different skills combine to enable effective thinking.
Three allow us to fully understand a problem; three more give us the tools to solve it. Together, these six skills make up the **PACIER** model of critical thinking. They are:

ANALYSIS – understanding how an argument is built
EVALUATION – exploring the strengths and weaknesses of an argument
INTERPRETATION – understanding issues of meaning

CREATIVE THINKING – coming up with new ideas and fresh connections
PROBLEM-SOLVING – producing strong solutions
REASONING – creating strong arguments

To find out more, visit **WWW.MACAT.COM.**

CRITICAL THINKING AND *CENTURIES OF CHILDHOOD*

Primary critical thinking skill: PROBLEM-SOLVING
Secondary critical thinking skill: INTERPRETATION

In *Centuries of Childhood*, the French historian Philippe Ariès offers a fundamentally fresh interpretation of what childhood is and what the institution means for society at large. Ariès's core idea is that 'childhood,' as we understand it today – a special time that requires special efforts and resources – is an invention of the 17th century, and that before that date children were in effect thought of as small adults. This led him to a re-evaluation of sources that suggested a second, crucial, conclusion: the idea that these competing visions of childhood were the products of two very different conceptions of human society.

An earlier, essentially communal, social ideal, Ariès wrote, had been supplanted by a society far more family-centric and hence inward-facing. In his view, moreover, this increased focus on childhood posed a direct challenge to a well-entrenched social order. 'One is tempted to conclude,' he wrote, 'that sociability and the concept of the family were incompatible, and could develop only at each other's expense.'

This revolutionary thesis, which has inspired and infuriated other historians in roughly equal measure, was made possible by Ariès's determination to understand the meaning of the evidence available to him and highlight problems of definition that others had simply glossed over, making *Centuries of Childhood* an important example of the critical thinking skill of interpretation.

ABOUT THE AUTHOR OF THE ORIGINAL WORK

Philippe Ariès was born in France in 1914. He wanted to be a university professor but did not pass the necessary exams, so he worked in business and journalism. He was a royalist and politically conservative, and his early work focused on what he saw as the decay in French society. Ariès called himself a 'Sunday historian,' proud of writing outside the university system in his spare time. After helping to launch the discipline of childhood studies, he was finally granted an academic appointment at the prestigious École des Hautes Études en Sciences Sociales in Paris in 1977. Ariès died in 1984 at the age of 69.

ABOUT THE AUTHORS OF THE ANALYSIS

Eva-Marie Prag holds a dual masters degree in international history from the University of Columbia and the London School of Economics.

Dr Joseph Tendler received his PhD from the University of St Andrews. He is the author of *Opponents of the Annales School*.

ABOUT MACAT

GREAT WORKS FOR CRITICAL THINKING

Macat is focused on making the ideas of the world's great thinkers accessible and comprehensible to everybody, everywhere, in ways that promote the development of enhanced critical thinking skills.

It works with leading academics from the world's top universities to produce new analyses that focus on the ideas and the impact of the most influential works ever written across a wide variety of academic disciplines. Each of the works that sit at the heart of its growing library is an enduring example of great thinking. But by setting them in context – and looking at the influences that shaped their authors, as well as the responses they provoked – Macat encourages readers to look at these classics and game-changers with fresh eyes. Readers learn to think, engage and challenge their ideas, rather than simply accepting them.

WAYS IN TO THE TEXT

KEY POINTS

- Philippe Ariès (1914–84) was a French historian of European history in the early modern* period—the late 1500s to the late 1800s.

- His book *Centuries of Childhood* argues that our modern idea of childhood was invented in the seventeenth century; until this point, children, who were then considered to be small adults, were marginal to society.

- The book continues to drive research into family and childhood history.

Who Was Philippe Ariès?

Philippe Ariès, the author of *L'Enfant et la vie familiale sous l'ancien régime* (published in English in 1962 as *Centuries of Childhood: A Social History of Family Life*) was born in 1914 in the Gironde region of southwest France. His parents raised him in Martinique,* a small island in the Caribbean Sea that forms part of the French Republic.

After failing the university professors' entrance exam (the *agrégation*),* Ariès decided to work for his family's fruit-importing company; he also took jobs as a journalist throughout his life. Ariès referred to himself as a "Sunday historian" because he wrote history at the weekends. This was before his 1977 appointment to the prestigious École des Hautes Études en Sciences Sociales (School of Advanced

Studies in the Social Sciences), where he taught and conducted research.

His most famous book, *Centuries of Childhood*, was first published in French in 1960. In the book, Ariès responded to widespread public debates in France about family planning, teenage pregnancy, sexual freedom, and education. It was topical from the outset; Ariès was prepared to get involved in public debate in France, even if those debates could be divisive.

Centuries of Childhood also showed that Ariès was motivated by the notion that history could help us understand the present. He wanted to show how family life had developed, thanks to new ideas that started to emerge in the seventeenth century. In rejecting the idea that the family in its modern form had always existed, he opposed the commonly held belief that nuclear families were in decline.

Ariès was a royalist* (a supporter of the French monarchy deposed in the eighteenth century) with an intellectual approach, writing from an unorthodox conservative* perspective, and in *Centuries of Childhood* he produced a work of social criticism and scholarly history. He felt that what he considered to be the healthy social character of France in the Middle Ages* (roughly, the fifth century to the beginning of the fifteenth century) was in decline, and he opposed the increasing power of governments to shape people's lives.

What Does *Centuries of Childhood* Say?

Centuries of Childhood claims that childhood as we know it did not exist in the Middle Ages, and that the modern idea of childhood was invented in the seventeenth century when it came to be understood as a distinct phase of development. The notion of childhood included the need for education, family life, and preparation for adulthood. This idea survives with greater power than ever today.

Ariès argues that the invention of childhood created new institutions. Because children needed to learn how to think and behave, they required a new kind of education, which spread rapidly from the eighteenth century onward. The goal of this education was to teach children how to read and to write, and to behave according to norms of social custom. However, as families focused more on nurturing children, they tended to deprioritize public life* that took place outside the home. This contrasted with the Middle Ages, during which time, Ariès believes, public life reigned supreme.

This idea matters to scholars because it showed how changes in attitudes toward children and the family had consequences for the relationship between private and public life. It also led to the start of a new field of research in social history* that drew on many different academic disciplines and is now known as childhood studies.* Social history aims to record the experience of everyday people, rather than the actions of monarchs or statesmen. Ariès's work served to popularize social history in general.

The idea of childhood also matters to the world at large, as Ariès provides a formidable example of how to question the world in which we live, to better understand it. Ariès was inspired by developments in French history studies in the twentieth century that responded to new social and demographic* shifts. In particular, he focused on the effects of the huge number of children born to the generation after World War II* (1939–45).

Ariès's work continues to attract scholars' attention and prompts new research even now. Recent publications have extended Ariès's focus from Europe to the world, such as *The Global History of Childhood Reader* by Heidi Morrison (2012). Google Scholar, which indexes scholarly literature in an array of journals and disciplines, showed that scholars have cited *Centuries of Childhood* more than 7,500 times.

Why Does *Centuries of Childhood* Matter?
Much more than a history of childhood, *Centuries of Childhood*

provides a provocative, fresh way of viewing childhood, and the issues it addresses remain open to debate. What is childhood? What are young people's educational needs? What roles should the family play in society?

Ariès's answers to those questions highlight a powerful way of explaining the world. In *Centuries of Childhood* he argues that our ideas shape the world and the way we live our lives. The lives of individuals and groups, then, are controlled by these ideas. The key to controlling and shaping our destiny is to understand what he referred to as the history of mentalities,* or unconscious mind-sets, from which ideas grow. He points out that, for the historian, this requires adequate sources to decipher those mind-sets—which may present difficulties.

Centuries of Childhood also provides a model for considering complex social developments across different fields of study, from anthropology* (the study of human beings, particularly our societies and culture) to biology* (the study of living things) and beyond. Although we tend to think of the family in terms of biological fact, the "family" is also a concept with a changing history of its own.

Ariès reminds us to consider how the young and old relate to one another, which is especially important in countries facing aging populations with a dropping birth rate, and he focuses on the importance of large-scale organizations in the study of ideas as causes of social change. Such organizations could be societies, companies, or charities, which all operate according to a particular set of ideas.

Centuries of Childhood matters, first and foremost, because it provides a key to analytical thought, encouraging readers to break down accepted ideas and customs and to analyze each of their parts. In doing so, it offers a powerful proposition: that, as with the idea of "childhood," the world is not necessarily as it may seem.

SECTION 1
INFLUENCES

MODULE 1
THE AUTHOR AND THE HISTORICAL CONTEXT

KEY POINTS

- *Centuries of Childhood* remains a deeply influential text on studies of childhood.*

- Philippe Ariès's fascination with, and nostalgia for, France in the Middle Ages*—the fifth to the fifteenth centuries— influenced the direction of his studies more than anything else.

- Debates about the function in society of the family in 1940s France focused Ariès's mind on the evolving nature of childhood.

Why Read This Text?

Philippe Ariès's *Centuries of Childhood: A Social History of Family Life* traces the concept of childhood from the late Middle Ages* (1301–1500) to modern times, through sources such as diaries, paintings, games, and school lessons. Ariès's principal argument is that the contemporary notion of childhood is a relatively recent invention, involving the relocation of the child from the margins of the family to its center. The book became the founding text in a new field of childhood history, which for many years revolved around Ariès's controversial claim that "childhood did not exist" in medieval* society.[1] There is a consensus among modern scholars that, in this debate, Ariès was roundly defeated.[2]

So influential has Ariès's work proved to be that *Centuries of Childhood* continues to set the agenda for childhood studies,* and looks likely to do so for the foreseeable future. Childhood studies is a recent discipline drawing on fields such as psychology* (the study of

> ❝ In 1945 the difficult emergence of French society from yet another decimating war with Germany was also an awakening to the urgency of social change. It was no longer a political option but a national necessity. ❞
>
> Rod Kedward, *La Vie en Bleu: France and the French since 1900*

the human mind and behavior), history, sociology* (the study of social behavior and society), anthropology* (the study of human culture and society as expressed by human behavior), and medical science; for people engaged in this field, childhood is considered necessary to the full understanding of human life.

While many of the beliefs about childhood that Ariès identified in mid-twentieth-century France have changed or look vastly different in other parts of the world, the fundamental movement of the child from the margins of the family to its center seems even more evident today than in 1960. Similarly, the separation between our public* and private lives that Ariès identified appears truer than ever.[3]

Author's Life

Ariès was born in 1914 to a middle-class Roman Catholic* family in the Gironde region in southwest France, where his family had deep roots although he was raised on the Caribbean island of Martinique,* where his mother was born. Growing up in a former colony far removed from the French mainland, Ariès was deeply influenced by his parents' image of "Old France" (that is, pre-Revolutionary* France).[4]

In his youth Ariès had hoped to become a professional historian, but after he failed his *agrégation** (civil-service exam) in 1939 and again in 1941, he resigned himself to pursue his interests outside the academic world. He would go on to work at a tropical-fruit company and as a journalist for most of his life, pursuing his passion for history on the weekends. The notion of being a "Sunday historian" would later become an important part of Ariès's self-styled image as a reactionary* (someone who favors a return to ideas of the past).

He was proud of working outside of, and in resistance to, the university system, which was dominated by republican* scholars who worked as salaried employees of the ministry of education.[5] As a royalist,* Ariès wanted his histories to focus on medieval France and French society—a reaction against the close ties between the republican government and republican scholars.

For much of his adult life, and especially in his youth, Ariès was openly supportive of right-wing political movements. As a student of history and geography at the University of Grenoble and the University of Paris, Ariès joined his university's branch of the far-right organization Action Française.* He objected to the curriculum of the Third Republic* (the period of French government from 1870 that was defeated by Nazi* Germany in 1940) and became interested in political journalism.

Charles Maurras,* a strong presence in right-wing intellectual circles in the 1930s for his critique of the state and society, influenced Ariès. During World War II,* Ariès also entered the orbit of Daniel Halévy,* a French Jewish intellectual and self-declared supporter of the extreme right. Halévy supported the regime of Vichy France,* the government that cooperated with the Nazis following the German invasion in World War II, after spending his youth as a fierce supporter of the republican cause.[6] Action Française, Maurras, and Halévy all swayed Ariès to think critically about accepted norms of French society, and in particular the sanctity of education and family life.

Author's Background

Influenced by the public debate in Vichy France about the alleged crisis in the institution of the French family, Ariès started researching the alleged moral and biological decay of the French population in 1943. This "decay" arose from the actual stagnation of the French population: from the end of the nineteenth century its growth had slowed as the birthrate fell, and, on average, the population had aged.[7] Ariès contended that the decline of the French population was the result of conscious decisions by married couples with regard to family planning.

Debates about family life continued into the postwar period. In the 1950s and 1960s, when *Centuries of Childhood* was published, the debate's focus had shifted toward issues of birth control as campaigns were being waged against a law from 1920 that made abortion and contraception illegal.[8] For this reason, family and children remained important topics for debate for Ariès and in France.[9]

His early research resulted in the 1948 book *Histoire des populations françaises* (*History of the French Population*), which examined the impact of increases in contraceptive practice and family planning on family life. From this, Ariès identified the emergence of a new model of the family that was centered on children. This laid the foundation for his most recognized book, *Centuries of Childhood*, which documents the rise of the modern nuclear family*—two parents and one or more children.[10]

NOTES

1   Philippe Ariès, *Centuries of Childhood: A Social History of Family Life*, trans. Robert Baldick (New York: Vintage Books, 1962), 128.

2   Patrick H. Hutton, *Philippe Ariès and the Politics of French Cultural History* (Amherst: University of Massachusetts Press, 2004), 4.

3   Adam Phillips, introduction to Philippe Ariès, *Centuries of Childhood*, trans. Robert Baldick (London: Pimlico, 1996), 10.

4   Hutton, *Philippe Ariès and the Politics of French Cultural History*, 21.

5   William R. Keylor, *Academy and Community: The Foundation of the French Historical Profession* (Cambridge, MA: Harvard University Press, 1975), 12–13.

6   Hutton, *Philippe Ariès and the Politics of French Cultural History*, 79.

7   Hutton, *Philippe Ariès and the Politics of French Cultural History*, 82.

8   Rod Kedward, *La Vie en Bleu: France and the French since 1900* (London: Allen Lane, 2005), 95.

9   Hutton, *Philippe Ariès and the Politics of French Cultural History*, 63.

10 Hutton, *Philippe Ariès and the Politics of French Cultural History*, 83.

MODULE 2
ACADEMIC CONTEXT

KEY POINTS

- Historical thought after World War II* (1939–45) turned away from political and military history toward economic and social history.*

- This movement focused on a broader study of ordinary people's lives.

- Working from the fringes of the academic community, Philippe Ariès promoted cultural history,* a type of social history examining how, historically, people's behavior reflects their culture.

The Work in its Context

In the period following World War II, during which Philippe Ariès wrote *Centuries of Childhood: A Social History of Family Life,* French historians' approaches began to alter. The war itself had prompted historians to reflect on their methods and aims—during the conflict, some had applied their research to assist the occupying Nazi* regime and the government of Vichy France* that collaborated with it; others opposed the Nazis. In the aftermath of combat, many questioned whether this political engagement had been a legitimate activity for scholars.[1]

The intellectual environment among historians was also changing. World War II further stimulated attention to social and economic history, as opposed to political and military matters, a turn that had begun in the 1920s. Since the late-nineteenth century, historians had sought to move away from the practice of using history to reinforce political positions or movements,[2] for example an excessive focus on

> ❝ Philippe Ariès must be counted among the most original French historians of the twentieth century. Building on his early work in historical demography, he became a pioneering scholar in the new cultural history, a focus of historians' interest from the 1960s to the 1980s. ❞
>
> Patrick H. Hutton, "Philippe Ariès (1914–1984)" in *French Historians 1900–2000*

the growth of political liberty since the French Revolution* of 1789–99 by historians who supported the goals of the revolution might be an example of history being used for political ends. Successive generations of historians believed that history should not only study political events, but should consider social developments more generally.[3]

The study of social and economic history became more important after World War I* (1914–18): the conflict had stimulated wide-ranging social change, to which historians responded. New disciplines emerged in the late-nineteenth century, such as sociology,* anthropology,* and ethnography.* Together with scholars working in these areas, historians began to look away from conventional histories of governments and nations toward people, communities, and their customs.

Overview of the Field

In 1929, two French historians launched *Annales d'histoire économique et sociale* (Annals of Economic and Social History), a scholarly journal that rejected the tradition of focusing largely on political, diplomatic, or military history. The journal led to the formation of what became known as the *Annales* school,* an influential movement focused on social history. The journal's founders, Lucien Febvre* and Marc

Bloch,* and their successors such as Fernand Braudel*—a contemporary of Ariès—emphasized the fundamental importance of studying the history of ordinary people's lives. They also provided examples of how to do this in their historical research, which focused on the early modern period*[4] (roughly 1500 until the French Revolution of 1789–99).

During the period between World War I and World War II, the *Annales* school was not alone in its concern with the lives of ordinary people. The French historian Ferdinand Lot* and others brought a similar focus to the study of the Middle Ages.*[5] French historians of the modern period such as Jacques Droz* wrote about all sections of society by examining the history of ideas.[6]

Childhood as a field of cultural study* remained of little importance during the mid-twentieth century, and it continued to be studied through physiological,* psychological,* and cognitive* theoretical models—that is, based on physical, emotional, and intellectual factors. These models became dominant in the early part of the century, based on the work of the Austrian thinker Sigmund Freud,* the founder of the therapeutic and theoretical methods of psychoanalysis.* Freud believed that childhood experiences, including traumatic experiences and sexual awakenings, informed later intellectual development. Despite this interest by psychologists and related fields, "childhood" was not seen as a topic for historians to tackle, or thought of as an idea with its own history.

Academic Influences

Ariès was strongly supportive of the calls by *Annales* historians and others to write a new kind of social and economic history, feeling that the old histories recounting the advance of democracy and liberty had become an outdated "religion of progress" shattered by World War II. The rise of the culture of mass consumption—shopping and spending as a cultural force—also focused Ariès's mind, and he felt he could contribute to public debates about new social developments, informed by the study of the past.[7]

The major difference between Ariès and the *Annales* historians was one of ideology. Ariès's sympathies lay firmly with conservative* Roman Catholic* politics that stressed the importance of community rather than mass societies over which governments imposed their values. He opposed abortion, which had remained a topic of debate in France since being banned in 1920. Ariès referred to himself as "truly reactionary,"*[8] which implies that he sought a return to the ways of the past, yet he participated in a major shift toward a new social and economic model in the study of French history.

In part because his career as a historian began by working in his spare time, Ariès maintained his independence from scholarly influences. He became a friend of Louis Chevalier* (a historian of demographic*—population-focused—change) through the very conservative historian Daniel Halévy.* Writing about France prior to the French Revolution with some fondness,[9] the three of them stood apart from the *Annales* historians (although Ariès also had ties with Robert Mandrou* and Georges Duby,* two historians of the Annales school).[10]

NOTES

1   Jens Qvortrup, ed., *Childhood Matters: Social Theory, Practice and Politics* (Aldershot: Avebury, 1994), 6.

2   Roy Lowe, "Childhood through the Ages," in *An Introduction to Early Childhood Studies*, ed. Trisha Maynard and Nigel Thomas (London: Sage Publications, 2004), 22.

3   Joseph Tendler, *Opponents of the Annales School* (Basingstoke: Palgrave Macmillan, 2013), 16.

4   André Burgière, *The Annales School: An Intellectual History*, trans. Jane Marie Todd (Ithaca, NY: Cornell University Press, 2009), 2–3.

5   Tendler, *Opponents of the Annales School*, 55–6.

6   Joseph Tendler, "Jacques Droz (1909–1998)," in *French Historians 1900–2000: New Historical Writing in Twentieth Century France*, ed. Philip Daileader and Philip Whalen (Oxford: Blackwell, 2010), 164–79.

7   Patrick H. Hutton, *Philippe Ariès and the Politics of French Cultural History* (Amherst: University of Massachusetts Press, 2004), 11.

8   Philippe Ariès and Michel Winock, *"L'Enfant à travers les siècles"* (The Child through the Centuries), L'Histoire 19 (January 1980): 86.

9   Tendler, *Opponents of the Annales School*, 68.

10 Hutton, *Philippe Ariès and the Politics of French Cultural History*, 34.

MODULE 3
THE PROBLEM

KEY POINTS

- Following World War II,* the key question preoccupying historians remained the same as in the nineteenth century: how to write about the past as it really had been.

- Historians in France approached this by focusing on social, economic, and cultural histories of ordinary people through the practice of writing what came to be known as "social history."*

- Philippe Ariès took up and developed this cultural approach to history, applying it specifically to ideas of family and childhood.

Core Question

Historians in twentieth-century France at the time Philippe Ariès wrote *Centuries of Childhood* searched for the best way to capture the past and bring it to life. They thought knowledge of the past and how society evolved over time could create better ways of living in the present. Lucien Febvre,* one of the cofounders of the French scholarly movement known as the *Annales* school* of history, for example, described history as the "science of man in time," transforming the way we see the world.[1]

The core issue Ariès addressed has two interdependent parts. First, how has the concept of childhood changed from the Middle Ages* until the present day? This question is linked not only to the history of the family, but to an understanding of modern society. It assumes that our modern idea of childhood has more to do with history than with biology.*

Second, Ariès and his colleagues focused on a question still

> **❝** The idea of family appeared to be one of the great forces of our time. I then went on to wonder, not whether it was on the decline, but whether it had ever been as strong before, and even whether it had been in existence for a long time. **❞**

Philippe Ariès, *Centuries of Childhood: A Social History of Family Life*

debated by historians: how best can the past be studied? Traditionally, historians had focused on wars, politics, and famous people. However, Ariès, along with members of the *Annales* school, believed they could provide a fuller understanding of history by studying and writing about ordinary people. This approach is a necessity for studying childhood and the family, as these are topics that would not ordinarily arise in traditional historical accounts.

The Participants

The debate centered on how the past could best be studied "scientifically." The *Annales* historian Fernand Braudel* encouraged the study of the "long duration" (a term he first used in a 1958 article to describe long-range developments and trends, although the idea had been central to his work since 1949.)[2] In the article, Braudel emphasized that historians should first study wide-ranging periods in the past, then analyze medium and short-term developments. "For me," Braudel wrote, "history is the sum of all possible histories—a collection of jobs and points of view of yesterday, today and tomorrow."[3]

Not all scholars shared his perspective. The anthropologist* Claude Lévi-Strauss* argued directly with Braudel in a landmark debate of the post-World War II era, stating instead that it remained important to study small groups of people over a short time period.[4] Historians also shared Lévi-Strauss's view that Braudel ignored the experiences of past people, by prioritizing long-term processes that were not the direct result of individual human efforts—from geographical trends to economic structures and demographic trends. Emmanuel Le Roy Ladurie,* for example, argued that human action is determined more by mentalities* (people's unconscious ideas about the world) than by anything else, even after he had tried to apply Braudel's long-, medium-, and short-term analysis.[5]

The debates between Braudel and others reflected a general development in the humanities* in France after World War II. Humanities scholars—academics in a wide range of disciplines including history, sociology,* literature, and languages—adopted scientific methods that enabled them to study subjects only scientists had considered previously. In this way, historians and their colleagues made history the "corridor" connecting the entire "science of society."[6]

The Contemporary Debate

Ariès introduced a new approach to the study of childhood that focused on the socially and culturally constructed *meaning* of childhood rather than on the child itself. He moved away from the notion of childhood as a collection of statements about children's physiology* (the physical nature), psychology* (their mind and behavior), and their cognitive* (intellectual) and speech development.

Ariès was moving in the same general direction as *Annales* historians such as Robert Mandrou* and Emmanuel Le Roy Ladurie, favoring the investigation of cultural factors. Ariès also seeks to clarify the present, explaining "this book on the family under the *ancien régime** is not the work of a specialist in that period, but of a demographic* historian who, struck by the original characteristics of the modern family, felt the need to go back into a more distant past to discover the limits of this originality."[7]

Centuries of Childhood does not cast itself as a scientific history in the sense that Braudel would have understood but, rather, as a trio of explorations of childhood, education, and family life. Ariès examines how people in the past saw the world, as displayed in their art, diaries, and shared stories, rather than by analyzing data about economic, social, demographic, and political changes. This reflects Ariès's political connections to the conservative* historian Daniel Halévy's* writing, and the value he places on producing elegantly written histories.

NOTES

1   Lucien Febvre, "Vers une autre histoire" (Toward Another History), *Revue de Métaphysique et de Morale* 63 (1949): 229, 233.

2   Fernand Braudel, "Histoire et sciences sociales: La longue durée" (History and the Social Sciences: The Long Duration), *Annales. Économies, Sociétés, Civilisations* 13, no. 4 (1958): 725–53.

3   Braudel, "Histoire et sciences sociales," 734.

4   Joseph Tendler, *Opponents of the Annales School* (Basingtoke: Palgrave Macmillan, 2013), 25–7.

5   Tendler, *Opponents of the Annales School*, 25.

6   Braudel, "Histoire et sciences sociales," 734.

7   Philippe Ariès, *Centuries of Childhood: A Social History of Family Life*, trans. Robert Baldick (New York: Knopf, 1962), 4.

MODULE 4
THE AUTHOR'S CONTRIBUTION

KEY POINTS

- Philippe Ariès argues that the notion of childhood is an invented idea with its own history.

- Ariès's line of argument made a considerable contribution to the study of mentalities* (that is, unconscious mind-sets).

- Ariès and others argued that our ideas shape the world, rather than the other way around.

Author's Aims

In *Centuries of Childhood: A Social History of Family Life*, Philippe Ariès asserted that children in the tenth century were considered to be little adults. He asked two interrelated questions in the book: "How did we come from that ignorance of childhood to the nineteenth-century idea that the family was centered around the child?" And, "How far does this evolution correspond to a parallel evolution of the concept people have of the family, the feeling they entertain toward it, the value they attribute to it?"[1]

Nobody had posed these two questions in print before. Conventional records of political archives and population records could not answer his questions. Ariès needed to provide an alternative account of the history of families and childhood, so he investigated the grounds for his conclusion that the family "had perhaps never before exercised so much influence over the human condition" using new and untapped sources such as private diaries and family paintings.[2]

From these sources, he considers the impact of childhood in society, the growth of educational institutions focused exclusively on children's needs, and the formalization of the family as the proper

> ❝ [Ariès] relied on a diverse set of documents …
> collecting all the signs of a new way of sorting out
> the social world. ❞
>
> André Burgière, *The Annales School: An Intellectual History*

source of care for children. Ariès argues that the increased focus on childhood posed a direct challenge to the social order. "One is tempted to conclude that sociability and the concept of the family were incompatible, and could develop only at each other's expense."[3]

Approach

Ariès applied an innovative historical method in developing his argument, emphasizing unconscious mind-sets or attitudes (which he referred to as "mentalities"). Ariès's overriding message was that with the change in relationship between children and parents in the seventeenth century came a concurrent change in society, as childhood became recognized as a distinct life phase.

Ariès had adopted a sociological* view of children within society; the term he used to indicate that his observations were based on population statistics was "demographic."* He studied "mentalities," the unconscious beliefs that inform how people think about the world; in this, he was particularly influenced by the pioneering French sociologist Émile Durkheim* and the ethnographer* Lucien Lévy-Bruhl.*

Ariès described the task of historians six years prior to publication of *L'Enfant et la vie familiale sous l'ancien régime* in 1960. "Historians," Ariès wrote, "try hard in particular to discover everything that past people had not known," while he felt it equally possible to write histories based on what past people did know.[4] He argued that discovering what past people had, and had not known, helps us to understand their ways of thinking. This is why he wrote a history of childhood: to discover how old the idea of family is, and whether or not its current domination of French society was historically unique.

Contribution in Context

Ariès's notion of mentality, resembles that of historians of the Annales school.* The *Annales* historian Robert Mandrou,* for example, explained in a book published in 1961: "every reconstitution of perceptions of the world incorporates a range of human facts and deeds, not just their words."[5]

Mandrou, however, was much less influential in the *Annales* school than Fernand Braudel.* In the 1950s and 1960s, Braudel's approach to history prioritized the environment and geography rather than human ideas. Mandrou and Braudel clashed on this very topic in 1962, and Mandrou resigned as secretary of the periodical *Annales d'histoire économique et sociale*, which was at the heart of the *Annales* school.

Ariès, like Mandrou, went much further than leading historians at the time in emphasizing the power of ideas to transform people's experience of the world. The work of these historians resembled that of scholars with whom they had little in common, personally or professionally, such as the historian Jacques Droz,* who argued that our ideas make the world what it is, rather than the world around us shaping our ideas.[6]

NOTES

1   Philippe Ariès, *Centuries of Childhood: A Social History of Family Life*, trans. Robert Baldick (New York: Knopf, 1962), 3.

2   Ariès, *Centuries of Childhood*, 10.

3   Ariès, *Centuries of Childhood*, 387.

4   Philippe Ariès, *Le Temps de l'histoire* (*The Time of History*) (Monaco: Éditions du Rocher, 1954), 282.

5   Robert Mandrou, *Introduction à la France moderne: Essai de psychologie historique 1500–1640* (*Introduction to Modern France: An Essay in Historical*

Psychology 1500–1640) (Paris: Albin Michel, 1961), x.

6   Joseph Tendler, "Jacques Droz (1909–1998)," in *French Historians 1900–2000: New Historical Writing in Twentieth Century France*, ed. Philip Daileader and Philip Whalen (Oxford: Blackwell, 2010), 174–5.

SECTION 2
IDEAS

MODULE 5
MAIN IDEAS

KEY POINTS

- The main themes of *Centuries of Childhood* are that childhood is an invention of the modern mentality,* that social institutions evolve in accordance with changing mentalities, and that social change is ultimately caused by changes of mentality.

- Ariès argues that the idea of childhood emerged in the seventeenth century and became an integral part of private life, changing the face of society in ways that continue to evolve today.

- This argument presents itself in three parts: as an analysis of attitudes toward children; of developments in educational institutions; and of the evolution of the nuclear family.*

Key Themes

The first key theme in Philippe Ariès's book *Centuries of Childhood: A Social History of Family Life* (published in English in 1962) is that phases of life such as childhood are the invention of an early modern* mentality that we have inherited today. This theme emphasizes the power of ideas to shape the way that people in the past and later generations live their life.

A second key theme is the way that unconscious ways of thinking (or mentalities) cause social change. Ariès's book represents a radical break from other works of social history* because it aligns social change with ideas and their histories, rather than factors such as economic, political, religious, climate, or population trends.

A third key theme integral to the book is how social institutions evolve with changing mentalities. Ariès starts by asserting that

> **"** In medieval society the idea of childhood did not exist; this is not to suggest that children were neglected, forsaken or despised. The idea of childhood is not to be confused with affection for children: it corresponds to an awareness of the particular nature of childhood, that particular nature which distinguishes the child from the adult, even the young adult. In medieval society this awareness was lacking. **"**
>
> Philippe Ariès, *Culture of Childhood: A Social History of Family Life*

"childhood" is an invention, moving on to examine how educational institutions cater to children, then examining how this changed society. For Ariès, the history of social institutions cannot be understood without the history of ideas.

Exploring the Ideas

Ariès's analysis of childhood as a relatively recent idea is consistent with his theme that phases of life are products of a way of thinking. When Ariès was writing, a commonsense view of life existed, grounded in biology,* according to which we all begin as children and transition through to the phase of adulthood. This idea, Ariès argues, resulted from how people viewed children, not from some fixed, external fact. The standard view before the seventeenth century, as reflected by the works of French intellectuals such as the philosopher Michel Montaigne* and the playwright Molière,* was that children were of no particular interest, being simply small people. As adults, "people could not allow themselves to become too attached to something that was regarded as a probable loss" owing to the limited life-spans many children had due to high child mortality rates.[1]

This only changed when people began to find the manners and ways of children endearing and deserving of particular attention or "coddling." This was the point at which people began to speak of "childhood" as we now know it "[freeing childhood] from both biology and law to become a value, a theme of expression, an occasion of emotion."[2]

Ariès also describes how this new mentality developed simultaneously with the emergence of a new education system.[3] The medieval* mentality regarding education saw it as "a technical school for the instruction of clerics" (church leaders) rather than young people.[4] In the eighteenth century, then, childhood required new educational institutions, something that was recognized by "those men of authority" who governed societies.[5] While initially reserved for male children of the elite, education gradually became a crucial element of the development of all children, particularly toward the early-nineteenth century.[6]

Ariès demonstrates how mentalities cause social change by showing that as childhood grew in importance, the family became an influential private institution. In medieval society, the socialization of individuals began from a young age, children mixing freely with their elders through work and play.[7] Over time, the nuclear family emerged, with two parents and one or more children as a self-contained unit. The family became a private vehicle to promote the interests of children as a group apart, with distinct needs. Thus, for Ariès, the invention of childhood in the seventeenth century was as much a liberation for the child, enabling their access to new pursuits, as it was a means of making him or her subject to the will of the family.[8]

Language and Expression

Ariès develops his argument according to a well-defined structure. He begins with "The Idea of Childhood" before moving to sections entitled "Scholastic Life," focusing on education, and "The Family," focusing on social change and the family.

Ariès's style is free from jargon. Referring to *l'ancien régime** (as the period before the French Revolution* is known), he explains that he did not write "as a specialist in [the *ancien régime*] period" for other specialists, but hoped instead to reach a wider public on an important topic.[9]

Ariès does not narrate his history chronologically from the fifteenth century to the present, instead dividing his material into sections by subject, and telling a story in each section. The tone throughout is both educational and conversational. For example, the "Summary"begins,"We have studied the beginnings and development of two views of childhood."[10] The language and tone reflect Ariès's unique position as a "Sunday historian"—Ariès's somewhat ironic self-description as an amateur—whose work gained some scholarly acceptance. It also indicates that he intended to reach the reading public as well as academics.

Ariès analyzed the idea of unconscious ways of thinking as a concept that, although not entirely new in the twentieth century, became increasingly influential.[11]

NOTES

1   Philippe Ariès, *Centuries of Childhood: A Social History of Family Life*, trans. Robert Baldick (New York: Knopf, 1962), 38–9.

2   Ariès, *Centuries of Childhood*, 10, 42.

3   Ariès, *Centuries of Childhood*, 323.

4   Ariès, *Centuries of Childhood*, 316.

5   Ariès, *Centuries of Childhood*, 322.

6   Ariès, *Centuries of Childhood*, 335.

7   Ariès, *Centuries of Childhood*, 72–3.

8   Ariès, *Centuries of Childhood*, 366.

9   Ariès, *Centuries of Childhood*, 1.

10 Ariès, *Centuries of Childhood*, 316.

11 André Burgière, *The Annales School: An Intellectual History*, trans. Jane

Marie Todd (Ithaca, NY: Cornell University Press, 2009), 7.

MODULE 6
SECONDARY IDEAS

KEY POINTS

- Philippe Ariès develops three secondary themes: the importance of using new and unconventional source material; the widening division in modern society between public* and private life; and the shortcomings of modern society.

- The first two address the core readership of *Centuries of Childhood*—scholars, students, and the reading public; the third is aimed at those who share Ariès's political convictions or who are interested in French political ideas.

- The division between public and private life, essential to his analysis of childhood and the family, is Ariès's most influential secondary idea.

Other Ideas

Secondary ideas in Philippe Ariès's *Centuries of Childhood: A Social History of Family Life* relate both to methodology—the means by which he conducts his research and analysis—and to his wider message about the development of Western society. Ariès's analysis of the history of childhood encouraged him to consult a wide and unusual collection of sources. This became a recognizable feature of his work and of the study of mentalities* and the history of ideas more generally.

The work looks closely at the growing separation between the private and public spheres of life since the Middle Ages.* Medieval* historians have referred to the period during the fifteenth century and beforehand as a "carnival" because of the way in which people of all ages, backgrounds, and classes mixed together in all kinds of activities

> 66 The history of modern manners can be reduced in part to [a] long effort ... to escape from a society whose pressure had become unbearable. The house lost the public character which it had ... in the seventeenth century, in favor of the club and the café, which in their turn have become less crowded. Professional and family life have stifled that other activity which once invaded the whole of life: the activity of social relations. One is tempted to conclude that sociability and the concept of the family were incompatible, and could develop only at each other's expense. 99
>
> Philippe Ariès, *Centuries of Childhood: A Social History of Family Life*

in each other's homes and in common spaces.[1] Ariès argues that the changing attitudes that emerged with the concept of childhood divided society into a private sphere for families and a public sphere, each with different interests.

Underlying these themes is the development of Ariès's critique of modern society. He suggests that the elevation of the family has destroyed medieval forms of being social, and that this has hurt social life in general. He also asserts that the growth of educational institutions that arose alongside the notion of childhood has encouraged increased government intervention in the lives of modern communities.

Exploring the Ideas

Ariès could not study childhood by using official government papers and records such as treaties, legislation, and contracts. With the exception of population statistics, these conventional documentary sources had little to do with children. He relies instead on sources such as diaries, paintings, games, and school lessons, as well as "scholars' memoirs."[2] Ariès set a strong precedent for other historians to follow him in writing histories based on people's mentalities, particularly in his original treatment of sources.[3]

Ariès used these sources of information to study the separation of the nuclear family* from public life that emerged throughout the eighteenth century. Ariès noted two opposing trends at work. The government was expanding its role in people's lives by dictating how children should prepare for adulthood through education. At the same time, people were increasingly investing their hopes in their personal lives rather than working to improve public life. The modern family, Ariès argued, "cuts itself off from the world."[4] All of the energy of society was now poured into children rather than into collective action.[5]

Ariès's social critique of modern society is certainly reflected in the book's closing lines: "The concept of family, the concept of class, and perhaps elsewhere the concept of race, appear as manifestations of the same intolerance toward variety, the same insistence on uniformity."[6] This secondary theme is essential to the political message Ariès proposes—that modern society interferes with sociability and is overly uniform.[7]

Overlooked

Rather than simply "move on" from Ariès, the historian Colin Heywood* has suggested that there is an opportunity to use his work as a starting point for new directions of study.[8]

First, the subject of gender* (the sum of attributes considered to represent identities such as "male" or "female") in Ariès's work remains underexplored. *Centuries of Childhood* has been cited in feminist* studies, from the Canadian-born social theorist Shulamith Firestone's* 1970 classic Dialectic of Sex, to more current studies of gender and family ("feminist" refers to the various intellectual and political perspectives associated with the struggle for equality between the sexes). But Ariès's own attitude toward women is not entirely clear.[9] Ariès addresses the role of women explicitly toward the end of the book, describing the woman's "deteriorating" place in the household from the fourteenth century onwards, with the husband being gradually established as the family's clear leader.[10] It was with this development that the family became "the social cell, the basis of the State, the foundation of the monarchy."[11] Ariès does not, however, state whether he approves of the husband being in charge.

Second, *Centuries of Childhood* can make a contribution to postcolonial studies* (meaning the inquiry into the various cultural and social legacies of colonialism).* Beginning in the sixteenth century, European nations sent settlers and soldiers to foreign countries to establish colonies and rule over the people who already lived there. Most of these former colonies became independent by the late-twentieth century. Among other customs, the European colonizers emphasized the need to discipline children in order for them to become moral, civilized adults. A postcolonial reading of the book could relate this to the civilizing trends of the Enlightenment,* the eighteenth- century period when intellectuals worked to end the abuses of the church and government and to increase freedom, tolerance, and reason. The Enlightenment provided much of the moral justification for continued colonization. Colonized people were often described as "children" who had to be civilized by Europeans before they could become ready for independence.[12]

NOTES

1   Adam Phillips, introduction to Philippe Ariès, *Centuries of Childhood: A Social History of the Family*, trans. Robert Baldick (London: Pimlico, 1996), 8.

2   Philippe Ariès, *Centuries of Childhood: A Social History of the Family*, trans. Robert Baldick (New York: Knopf, 1962), 5.

3   Patrick H. Hutton, *Philippe Ariès and the Politics of French Cultural History* (Amherst: University of Massachusetts Press, 2004), 89.

4   Philippe Ariès, *Centuries of Childhood*, trans. Robert Baldick (New York: Vintage Books, 1962), 406.

5   Ariès, *Centuries of Childhood*, 407.

6   Ariès, *Centuries of Childhood*, 411.

7   Ariès, *Centuries of Childhood*, 11.

8   Colin A. Heywood, *A History of Childhood: Children and Childhood in the West from Medieval to Modern Times* (Cambridge: Polity Press, 2001), 15.

9   See, for example, Naomi Miller and Naomi Yavneh, eds., *Gender and Early Modern Constructions of Childhood* (Farnham: Ashgate, 2011).

10 Ariès, *Centuries of Childhood*, 365.

11 Ariès, *Centuries of Childhood*, 365.

12 Alice L. Conklin, *A Mission to Civilize: The Republican Idea of Empire in France and West Africa, 1895–1935* (Redwood City, CA: Stanford University Press, 1997), 7–9.

MODULE 7
ACHIEVEMENT

KEY POINTS

- *Centuries of Childhood* shows how ways of thinking determine social change, and how the notion of childhood has changed modern society.
- Nobody had published a history of the idea of childhood before.
- Ariès's work came in for criticism for ignoring certain periods and for being vague in establishing timelines.

Assessing the Argument

In his *Centuries of Childhood: A Social History of Family Life* (published in English in 1962), Philippe Ariès tackled a largely unexplored topic, childhood, by means of a highly original historical method. Ariès referred to this approach as a history of mentalities,* and he sought to understand the everyday mind-set and experiences of ordinary people rather than the history of political decisions by kings and state leaders.

The fact that this approach has become so influential in the humanities* and social sciences shows that Ariès was successful. The prominent French philosopher and historian Michel Foucault* followed Ariès and the Annales school* historians who studied this kind of social history.* Foucault also started with a current issue and worked back to its origins, highlighting changes over time. In an obituary that Foucault wrote about Ariès, he described Ariès's method as searching for our social values in our collective attitudes, which had given us "the unexpected gift of original insight."[1]

Ariès clearly outlines the nature and the effects of the invention of childhood. In his conclusion, he notes "our world is obsessed by the

> **❝** *Centuries of Childhood* remains one of those books that, virtually on contact, sets the mind on fire. **❞**
>
> Stephen Metcalf, "Farewell to Mini-Me: The Fight over When Childhood Began

physical, moral, and sexual problems of childhood," a claim based on the many examples in the book.[2]

Achievement in Context

Ariès was the first to write about the concept of childhood based on the history of ideas, and he was one of the first to write about the nature of childhood and the family. This helped *Centuries of Childhood* to command a position of authority when it was first published in French in 1960, because it had no serious rivals.

In addition, Ariès offered a rereading of "Old (pre-Revolutionary)* France" based on the lives of ordinary people in his search for authentic alternatives to the modern way of life.[3] Ariès became one of the most influential historians in French history, particularly through promoting an idealized image of preindustrial French society.[4]

However, Ariès's original arguments can get in the way of understanding his key ideas. First, the historical analysis is flawed because he ignores certain sources and historical periods. For example, there is clear evidence that Europeans increased their social and psychological investment in children during the Renaissance,* the period in which Europe emerged from the Middle Ages* in the fourteenth through seventeenth centuries. This entire period is all but dismissed by Ariès as insignificant to the history of childhood.[5]

Second, the chronology is vague. The book sometimes identifies the fifteenth century and sometimes the seventeenth as the beginning of new ideas about childhood. Moreover, Ariès does not explain how the concept of childhood emerged as a distinct category.

Limitations

Centuries of Childhood responded to and added to debates about the family in mid-century France in particular, which invites the question: is this book relevant beyond Western Europe? The anthropologist Janet Hart* says that Ariès's argument "reflects the blithely Eurocentric* bias common to the discussion at that point."[6] In other words, she means Ariès assumes that European thinking is superior to that of other regions—an example of "Eurocentric" thought.

Such Eurocentrism is particularly glaring in parts of the book that mention educational practices in "Moslem" countries, what we would refer to today as Muslim countries, where Islam is the dominant religion.[7] In using this term, Ariès lumps together a large number of societies that in fact have different cultures, and his implication is that Muslim practices are backward.

Yet Ariès did not argue that modern European practices are superior—in fact, he criticizes the idea. His approach to history was influential in later research about the supposed universality of Western notions of childhood and family. Some recent research on childhood in China, Japan, and India, for example, is based on Ariès's argument that "childhood" does not have a universal meaning.[8]

NOTES

1   Patrick H. Hutton, "Late-Life Historical Reflections of Philippe Ariès on the Family in Contemporary Culture," *Journal of Family History* 26, no. 3 (July 2001): 405, doi: 10.1177/036319900102600305.

2   Philippe Ariès, *Centuries of Childhood: A Social History of the Family*, trans. Robert Baldick (New York: Knopf, 1962), 395.

3   Patrick H. Hutton, *Philippe Ariès and the Politics of French Cultural History* (Amherst: University of Massachusetts Press, 2004), xii.

4   Hutton, *Philippe Ariès and the Politics of French Cultural History*, ix.

5   Colin A. Heywood, *A History of Childhood: Children and Childhood in the West from Medieval to Modern Times* (Cambridge: Polity Press, 2001), 21.

6   Janet Hart, "Reading the Radical Subject: Gramsci, Glinos, and Paralanguages of the Modern Nation," in *Intellectuals and the Articulation of the Nation*, ed. Ronald Grigor Suny and Michael Kennedy (Ann Arbor: University of Michigan Press, 2001), 171–204.

7   Philippe Ariès, *Centuries of Childhood: A Social History of the Family*, trans. Robert Baldick (New York: Vintage Books, 1962), 138.

8   Anne Behnke Kinney, ed., *Chinese Views of Childhood* (Honolulu: University of Hawaii Press, 1995); Peter N. Stearns, *Childhood in World History* (New York: Routledge, 2006), 12–13.

MODULE 8
PLACE IN THE AUTHOR'S WORK

KEY POINTS

- Studying the demographic* and cultural evolution of modern society was Philippe Ariès's life's work.
- *Centuries of Childhood* marks a pivotal development from Ariès's early demographic studies into a broader concern with the relationship between private and public life.*
- Gaining only limited attention until its translation into English in 1962, *Centuries of Childhood* demonstrates the central themes of Ariès's work: the history of mentalities* and the analysis of social change.

Positioning

When Philippe Ariès's *L'Enfant et la vie familiale sous l'ancien régime* was published in France in 1960, Ariès was 46 years old and in the middle of his career as a historian. None of his work, before or after *Centuries of Childhood* (as it was titled in its English translation), would attain the same level of influence as his breakthrough book. However, although *Centuries of Childhood* paved the path to Ariès's recognition in the academic world and beyond, the book is best understood as part of Ariès's larger body of innovative historical studies.

Centuries of Childhood represented a thematic move away from his earlier work, which focused on studying statistical population trends, and into the study of attitudes toward life. This led to another influential study, of attitudes toward death, that also contributed to Ariès's considerable fame.

That work was *L'Homme devant la mort* (1977), literally "man in front of death," published in English in 1981 with the title *The Hour of Our Death*. In this book, Ariès investigated Western attitudes toward

> **"** Few readers of *L'Enfant et la vie familiale,* whether professional or lay, were aware of its groundwork in Ariès's earlier demographic research into changing attitudes toward sexuality and spousal relations. **"**
>
> Patrick H. Hutton, "Philippe Ariès (1914–1984)" in *French Historians 1900–2000*

death and mourning, arguing that traditions tying the individual to his community developed over two millennia had been forgotten in the twentieth century. Ariès said modern people "banished the idea of evil, tamed nature, discarded the afterlife, doused the last embers of communal spirit—and in the process restored death to its savage state."[1]

Together, *Centuries of Childhood* and *The Hour of Our Death* led Ariès to his final project, in which he sought to trace the history of private life that he had only hinted at in *Centuries of Childhood.* While Ariès died in 1984, too soon to realize the project, his colleagues at the prestigious École des Hautes Etudes en Sciences Sociales* made it a reality. A five-volume work, *Histoire de la vie privée* (*History of Private Life*) was published between 1985 and 1987.

Integration

Centuries of Childhood reveals just one aspect—childhood/family history—of Ariès's broader interest in modern society and the history of private life. According to the American historian Patrick H. Hutton,* *Centuries of Childhood* does not fully capture Ariès's treatment of these topics in his other works, which were comprehensive and filled with subtle insights.[2] However. it does capture the spirit of Ariès's life's work: to reexamine the present and better understand contemporary culture by studying what it preserves of previous ways of life, and what it has destroyed.

Ariès was a rebellious historian from the outset, criticizing the scholarly works of the Third Republic* (the period of French government from 1870 until 1940) during his time as a university student and member of the right-wing organization Action Française* in the 1930s. His contempt for prevailing scholarship led to his writing *Le Temps de l'histoire* (*The Times of History*) in 1954, which reviewed French historical writing in a way that foreshadowed the deconstructionist* approach of historical scholarship toward the end of the twentieth century.[3] In other words, from early in his career, Ariès had sought to dismantle or "deconstruct" accepted interpretations of social norms and customs.

Significance

Centuries of Childhood is Ariès's most important work, combining his history of mentalities (that is, unconscious mindsets or attitudes) approach with his previous demographic work, and his early interest in public–private life distinctions. Without the book, his international reputation would not have risen to the heights it still enjoys today.

Following the English translation in 1962, scholars, child psychologists,* and the reading public in the United States were fascinated by the historical insights Ariès provided about the concept of the family. After Ariès achieved scholarly fame in the US, he became equally recognized in his home country, France, and soon became known as one of the most influential French historians of the twentieth century.

Moreover, *Centuries of Childhood* presented a radical thesis* that guided Ariès throughout his career, and that remains contested today. As the French historian André Burgière* states, the book "showed change to be a movement internal to society, or rather, to consciousness, lending credence to the idea that social organization is not structured by its institutions, by the distribution of its assets and interests, but by its ways of thinking."[4]

NOTES

1   *Wilson Quarterly*, "Philippe Ariès: Mentality as History," *Wilson Quarterly* 5, no. 1 (Winter 1981): 102–4, http://www.jstor.org/stable/40256047.

2   Patrick H. Hutton, *Philippe Ariès and the Politics of French Cultural History* (Amherst: University of Massachusetts Press, 2004), 93.

3   Hutton, *Philippe Ariès and the Politics of French Cultural History*, xi.

4   André Burgière, *The Annales School: An Intellectual History*, trans. Jane Marie Todd (Ithaca, NY: Cornell University Press, 2009), 178.

SECTION 3
IMPACT

MODULE 9
THE FIRST RESPONSES

KEY POINTS

- *Centuries of Childhood* immediately launched lively discussions, with psychologists and sociologists* applying the concepts to their own work, while many historians were critical.

- Much of the criticism focused on the book's negative conclusions about the notion of childhood, and its incomplete social analysis.

- While Philippe Ariès never directly responded to his critics, he did say that *Centuries of Childhood* could be improved by further study of customs such as infanticide* (the killing of infants) and religious baptism (the ritual of acceptance into the Christian Church) before the seventeenth century.

Criticism

Philippe Ariès's *Centuries of Childhood: A Social History of Family Life* enjoyed significant praise, particularly on its translation into English in 1962.[1] But it soon encountered criticism, particularly from historians. Two prominent researchers, the American social theorist Lloyd deMause* and the English historian Lawrence Stone,* agreed that childhood was an invented idea, but advanced influential critiques of Ariès's attitude toward childhood as a concept.

DeMause, who established the journal *History of Childhood Quarterly* and edited one of the first major collections of scholarship on the subject, *The History of Childhood* (1974), disagreed with Ariès's pessimistic interpretation of childhood, and focused on child psychology.* He insisted that the focus on childhood as a distinct life

> ❝ If one seeks to reconstruct the status of the child at any given time on the basis of Ariès's assorted evidence, one meets vagueness and even inconsistency. ❞
>
> Irene Quenzler Brown, review of *Centuries of Childhood*

phase since the seventeenth century had improved children's lives, and that of society, immeasurably.[2]

Lawrence Stone, by contrast, argued that "for all its seminal brilliance," *Centuries of Childhood* raised basic questions about methods, timelines, reliability of data, and the validity of Ariès's claim that the emergence of childhood had helped to shape the course of history. Stone concluded that the book was "a history of French schools, and of upper-class and middle-class parents and children that lacks the necessary historical context of time, place, class, and culture."[3] Ariès's social analysis, in other words, was incomplete.

Responses

Ariès never responded directly to his critics. Instead, reflecting on *Centuries of Childhood* in the 1980s, he described the experience of a historian in "the freshness of discovery," an experience that could blind historians to flaws in their argument.[4] Although he admitted that he had come to see his own ideas more clearly with the passage of time, Ariès held on to the belief that childhood was an invented idea and its consequences had changed society, often for the worse.

Ariès offered indirect responses in the form of four suggestions for improving *Centuries of Childhood*:

- First, he would study more closely the widely tolerated practice of infanticide to discover more about attitudes to children before the invention of childhood (as he claimed) in the seventeenth century.
- Second, he would investigate the history of the Christian

practice of religious baptism, to see how this reflected historical attitudes toward children.
- Third, he would study children's gravestones and other monuments dedicated to infants over time.
- Finally, he would pay closer attention to domestic architecture as part of his study of the history of the family.[5]

Ariès made no apologies for his approach, which was guided by his own ideas and insights rather than by comprehensive research. He maintained that his selection from a very wide range of sources was more credible than a systematic and detailed analysis of a narrow range of more traditional sources. Ariès published articles and essays during the 1970s and 1980s that continued to develop his arguments about the nuclear family* and its fragile relationship with an emerging mass culture.[6]

Conflict and Consensus

The critical reception of *Centuries of Childhood* quickly took on a life of its own in the United States. Psychologists and sociologists applied the book's argument to their own experience with maturing children, and social historians either built upon his argument or discarded it entirely.[7]

There is no widespread agreement about the validity of *Centuries of Childhood*, which is as much a subject of debate today as it was in 1984, the year of Ariès's death. As Ariès himself wrote toward the end of his life, "The case [concerning the history of childhood] is far from closed … Let us hope that the scholarly energy devoted to the search is expended wisely, opening new areas of inquiry rather than burying itself under an endless sifting of old ideas."[8]

The absence of general agreement reflects both the continued evolution of childhood studies* and the ongoing social questions that frame any attempt to write a history of modern family life. The discipline of childhood and family studies is now well established, and combines work from psychology, demography,* history, and cultural studies* (an academic discipline in which culture is considered as a lived experience). But moral and social questions about family values and attitudes to children continue to be asked.[9]

NOTES

1   Patrick H. Hutton, *Philippe Ariès and the Politics of French Cultural History* (Amherst: University of Massachusetts Press, 2004), 93.

2   Lloyd deMause, ed., *The History of Childhood* (New York: Psychohistory Press, 1974), 1.

3   Lawrence Stone, "The Massacre of the Innocents," *New York Review of Books* (November 1974): 27.

4   Philippe Ariès, "The Sentimental Revolution," *Wilson Quarterly* (Autumn 1982): 47.

5   Ariès, "The Sentimental Revolution," 50–2.

6   Patrick H. Hutton, "Late-Life Historical Reflections of Philippe Ariès on the Family in Contemporary Culture," *Journal of Family History* 26, no. 3 (July 2001): 398, doi: 10.1177/036319900102600305.

7   Ariès, "The Sentimental Revolution," 47; Hutton, *Philippe Ariès and the Politics of French Cultural History*, 92.

8   Ariès, "The Sentimental Revolution," 52.

9   Hutton, "Late-Life Historical Reflections of Philippe Ariès on the Family in Contemporary Culture," 399.

MODULE 10
THE EVOLVING DEBATE

KEY POINTS

- Philippe Ariès's argument about the invention of childhood remains influential, but since the 1980s it has provoked criticisms that it is based on incomplete evidence.

- While no clear school of thought emerged directly from Ariès's research, his work fed into the efforts of the *Annales* school* to promote the history of mentalities* as a distinct approach to cultural history.*

- *Centuries of Childhood* has become a classic example of the methods used to study the history of changing ideas, as well as a founding text for childhood studies.

Uses and Problems

Philippe Ariès's *Centuries of Childhood: A Social History of Family Life* has, since the 1960s, catalyzed the study of childhood history. The American historian Margaret L. King* argues that the history of childhood has two parts. The mid-1960s to the mid-1980s was "the heroic era," when scholars explored the new subject of childhood history with sweeping theories, leading to numerous competing claims. From the mid-1980s to the present, a "filling-in" era addresses gaps in the literature of "the heroic era."[1]

Ariès's work remained central throughout both eras, and came in for criticism. The historian Adrian Wilson* made four points in a 1980 article:[2]

- Ariès's collection of evidence was almost exclusively based on pictures, stories, and examples, rather than data.
- The central argument about the historical development of

❝ While Ariès moved on to other projects, *Centuries* remained the reference point to which he was tethered by his critics, who have based their judgment of his authorship on their analysis of this text ❞

Patrick H. Hutton, *Philippe Ariès and the Politics of French Cultural History*

childhood was not related carefully, or at all, to Ariès's wider points about social change (family versus public life) or institutional change (public sphere versus school).

- Because of the vague timelines, any "given point in time (for example, the beginning of the seventeenth century) can variously be located as early, late, or in-between in the unfolding of the story."[3]
- Ariès was "present-minded" because in analyzing previous attitudes toward children, he simply recorded the absence of present attitudes, rather than studying the attitudes in place at the time.[4]

As the French-born literary historian Doris Desclais Berkvam* noted in the early 1980s, these shortcomings leave unanswered the question of whether there existed in the Middle Ages* "a consciousness of childhood so unlike our own that we do not recognize it."[5] The strengths of *Centuries of Childhood*—its original approach and broad claims—thus also became its weaknesses.[6]

Schools of Thought

Centuries of Childhood played an important role in popularizing the history of mentalities, or ways of thinking. Members of the Annales school such as the historians Georges Duby,* Jacques Le Goff,* and Robert Mandrou* also developed similar approaches, although they never went so far as Ariès to claim that ideas caused social change. The combined effect of this work by Ariès and by members of the Annales school helped to popularize this field of study among scholars in the 1960s and 1970s, and brought widespread recognition from the public.[7]

The American social theorist Lloyd deMause* and the English historian Lawrence Stone* can be identified with Ariès's approach, even though they criticized his findings. DeMause founded the scholarly periodical *History of Childhood Quarterly,* and edited one of the first major collections of scholarship on the subject, *The History of Childhood*. Stone also worked on family history and, like Ariès, paid some attention to the Annales school.[8]

But nothing that could be considered a school of thought was ever generated around Ariès or his work. This is in part because Ariès wrote history in his spare time, and was not associated with a university until his later years. The absence of a school of thought is also connected to the conservative* political attitudes revealed in *Centuries of Childhood,* as such attitudes did not command widespread support in 1960s France.

In Current Scholarship

The influence of *Centuries of Childhood* today is mostly confined to the field of childhood history—but this field has become so diverse that it is almost impossible to generalize about Ariès's role within it. While Ariès remains an important figure to many scholars of childhood history due to his status as the founder of the subdiscipline, his supporters may be limited to those who are fascinated by his broad interest in modern society.

The American historian Patrick H. Hutton,* a strong supporter, says we ought to pay more attention to Ariès's argument about the dangers of modern mass culture and the separation it creates between public* and private lives.[9] Ariès strongly believed that, as we increasingly dedicate our lives to the idea of a nuclear family,* we give up a potentially more meaningful existence as part of diverse and strong communities. Hutton argues that the debate around *Centuries of*

Childhood has overshadowed this part of the book and the important insights it offers.

The study retains its significance for those who see it as a "book to think with" due to Ariès's insightful and original ability to explain the problems of his time.[10]

NOTES

1   Margaret L. King, "Concepts of Childhood: What We Know and Where We Might Go," *Renaissance Quarterly* 60, no. 2 (Summer 2007): 371–407.

2   Adrian Wilson, "The Infancy of the History of Childhood: An Appraisal of Philippe Ariès," *History and Theory* 19, no. 2 (1980).

3   Wilson, "The Infancy of the History of Childhood," 136.

4   Wilson, "The Infancy of the History of Childhood," 139.

5   Doris Desclais Berkvam, "Nature and Norreture: A Notion of Medieval Childhood and Education," *Mediaevalia* 9 (1983): 165.

6   Wilson, "The Infancy of the History of Childhood," 152.

7   Joseph Tendler, *Opponents of the Annales School* (Basingstoke: Palgrave Macmillan, 2013), 38, 68.

8   Tendler, *Opponents of the Annales School*, 38.

9   Patrick H. Hutton, *Philippe Ariès and the Politics of French Cultural History* (Amherst: University of Massachusetts Press, 2004), ix.

10 Hutton, *Philippe Ariès and the Politics of French Cultural History*, 110–2.

IMPACT AND INFLUENCE TODAY

KEY POINTS

- *Centuries of Childhood* remains a classic study of childhood history and a key statement of the history of mentalities,* provoking new directions in scholarship.

- The key challenge posed by the book remains how to prove Ariès's assertion that childhood was an idea invented in the seventeenth century.

- Critics focus on parent–child relationships and evidence, but also reframe the question by looking at experiences of life from the children's points of view.

Position

Centuries of Childhood: A Social History of Family Life by Philippe Ariès continues to spark debate among scholars of childhood, and remains a landmark study in the history of mentalities.[1] It attracts attention from an array of fields such as medieval* history, art history,* sociology,* and child psychology.*

Scholars have continued to work to determine when the concept of childhood emerged. A 2007 collection of essays on childhood in the Middle Ages* shows widespread agreement that although parents felt love and concern for their children, the Middle Ages did not feature the sentimental glorification of childhood that is evident in many countries today. Yet these same accounts strongly disagree with Ariès that children had no special status at all.[2] This implies that while childhood in the Middle Ages may have been very different from today, other manifestations of childhood may very well have existed.[3]

Scholars have also investigated whether Ariès used the correct

> **"** A maverick, Philippe Ariès was the true precursor in France of the exploration of mentalities. **"**
>
> François Dosse, "Ariès, Philippe (Blois, 1914–Toulouse 1984)"

term by referring to the "invention" of childhood. The British historian Hugh Cunningham* notes that while Ariès does talk about "invention," he was actually referring to our contemporary idea of childhood, and not implying that parents in the past did not care for their children.[4] This confusion was not helped by Ariès's use of the word "discovery" to describe the emergence of modern childhood.

Interaction

Ariès's central claim that the notion of childhood is a recent invention continues to be controversial. The general public and scholars alike have difficulty accepting that childhood is an idea constructed from class, gender,* religion, and race, among other factors. The British historian Linda Pollock* still seeks to prove that the relationship between child and parent is universal and constant in nature.[5] Pollock's argument is consistent with the views of the American medieval historian Barbara Hanawalt,* who insists that Ariès's sources were not strong enough to prove his point.[6]

The British historian Nicholas Orme* speaks for many medieval historians when he attempts to disprove that our idea of childhood was invented in the way Ariès describes.[7] However, as Hugh Cunningham notes in his evaluation of the field of childhood studies, many of the criticisms made of *Centuries of Childhood* can be attributed to the widespread but faulty assumption that Ariès's stance "was a slur on the Middle Ages."[8] Ariès did not mean that medieval children were not loved, but rather that they were not pampered—for example, they were expected to work at an early age.

The Continuing Debate

This misunderstanding—that Ariès was suggesting parents did not care for their children during the Middle Ages—has led to significant studies of the history of parent–child relationships. Linda Pollock argued in the 1980s that parents have consistently shown grave concern for ill or dying children and that parental affection has remained constant throughout history.[9] That said, other scholars have challenged this, and the issue of adult–child relations, which was a source of early fascination in this academic field, remains unsettled.[10] This is evident from recent accounts such as Orme's 2001 book *Medieval Children*, which responds to Ariès's account of the nature of parental affection during that era. Orme refutes Ariès's position by using contemporary schoolbooks, journals, coroners' records, and even shoes to show that, in his view, childhood in the Middle Ages was almost identical to our modern experience of it.[11]

Scholars continue to respond to a lack of physical evidence for the existence of childhood in the Middle Ages. As most people in the early modern* period were illiterate, historians are often left to speculate. Alternative sources used by Ariès, such as paintings, address some of these concerns, but the American art historian Laurel Reed* recently argued that Ariès omitted important works that contradict his own thesis.* For example, *Portrait of Clarissa Strozzi* by the sixteenth-century Italian painter Titian* depicts a child with a puppy who seems to be experiencing childhood in a way that we would recognize today.[12] However, as with written sources, paintings were reserved for society's wealthiest members in the Middle Ages and early modern times. An increasing awareness of such limitations has led to more caution in making generalized claims about childhood in the past.

The most recent responses to Ariès's account have focused on the experiences of children. Arguing that the collective actions of children as drivers of historical change have been overlooked in previous studies, scholars such as Barbara Hanawalt and the American psychologist Lester Alston* have sought to reconstruct the lives of children through sources such as court documents and personal records.[13]

NOTES

1   André Burgière, *The Annales School: An Intellectual History*, trans. Jane Marie Todd (Ithaca, NY: Cornell University Press, 2009), 34.

2   Joel T. Rosenthal, ed., *Essays on Medieval Childhood: Responses to Recent Debates* (Donington: Shaun Tyas, 2007).

3   Ilana Krausman Ben-Amos, "Adolescence as a Cultural Invention: Philippe Ariès and the Sociology of Youth," *History of the Human Sciences* 8, no. 2 (May 1995): 82, doi: 10.1177/095269519500800204.

4   Hugh Cunningham, "Histories of Childhood," *American Historical Review* 103, no. 4 (1998): 1199.

5   Linda A. Pollock, *Forgotten Children: Parent–Child Relations from 1500 to 1900* (Cambridge: Cambridge University Press, 1983).

6   Barbara A. Hanawalt, *Growing Up in Medieval London: The Experience of Childhood in History* (Oxford: Oxford University Press, 1993), 440.

7   Nicholas Orme, *Medieval Children* (New Haven: Yale University Press, 2001).

8   Cunningham, "Histories of Childhood," 1197.

9   Pollock, *Forgotten Children*, 283.

10 William A. Corsaro, *The Sociology of Childhood* (London: Sage Publications, 2005), 81.

11 Orme, *Medieval Children*.

12 Hanawalt, *Growing up in Medieval London*, 440; Laurel Reed, "Art, Life, Charm and Titian's *Portrait of Clarissa Strozzi*," in *Childhood in the Middle Ages and the Renaissance: The Results of a Paradigm Shift in the History of Mentality*, ed. Albrecht Classen (Berlin: Walter de Gruyter, 2005), 355–71.

13 Hanawalt, *Growing up in Medieval London*; Lester Alston, "Children as Chattel," in *Small Worlds: Children and Adolescents in America, 1850–1950*, ed. Elliott West and Paula Petrik (Lawrence: University Press of Kansas, 1992), 208–31.

MODULE 12
WHERE NEXT?

KEY POINTS

- While some of Philippe Ariès's specific conclusions may be questioned today, *Centuries of Childhood* will continue to serve as a landmark study of childhood history.

- The continuing impact of *Centuries of Childhood* is due to its tendency to trigger debate about adult–child relations.

- *Centuries of Childhood* is a groundbreaking text because it presents a radical way of looking at the history of mentalities,* provides a new interpretation of modern social history,* and continues to encourage debate.

Potential

The British historian Colin Heywood,* a scholar of French history, argues that despite the important contribution made through the originality of Philippe Ariès's thought in *Centuries of Childhood: A Social History of Family Life*, his arguments are outdated.[1]

In Heywood's view, the debate about when the "discovery" of childhood took place has run its course and the text has served its purpose. While *Centuries of Childhood* had a "brilliant though controversial youth" followed by a "remarkably long career during adulthood," Heywood argues that it is time for it to "retire from active life."[2] Even this partial approval implies that *Centuries of Childhood* will remain a point of reference for family and childhood scholars.

According to Ariès in *Centuries of Childhood,* the purpose of history is to clarify our understanding of the world, and, by so doing, improve our lives. With regard to the fortunes of children, this task is enormous given the growth in child poverty, the suffering of children displaced

❝Philippe Ariès's *L'Enfant et la vie familiale sous l'ancien régime* (1960), better known to American readers as *Centuries of Childhood* (1962), is a revealing example of how a work of history, like one of art or literature, may take on a life of its own amongst its critics. Assessing its significance has become as much a matter of its readership as its authorship.❞

Patrick H. Hutton, *French Cultural History*

by war and afflicted by famine, and the problems of access to education for many children. The field of childhood studies* and the history of childhood and the family can reflect these problems of the contemporary world, as Ariès did in postwar France.

Future Directions

Childhood studies is a recognized field for scholars working across the world in subjects from psychology* through history and sociology* to anthropology* and medical science. These scholars believe that an understanding of childhood is necessary in order to understand humanity. This was demonstrated in 2002 by the formation of the Society for the History of Children and Youth, an international academic group that publishes a peer-reviewed journal. When a collection of nearly 30 scholarly works on childhood was published in 2012 as *The Global History of Childhood Reader*, the first chapter was an excerpt from *Centuries of Childhood*. Childhood studies are also a matter of continuing concern in society at large, as public debates rage about education, career prospects, the abuse of children by people in positions of power, and the exploitation of children in underpaid positions of employment.

Such is the scope of childhood studies today that, according to the historian Paula Fass,* childhood should be used to study the history of humankind as a whole.[3] Fass suggests that disciplines like neurobiology* (study of the biological processes and structures of the brain and the nervous system), anthropology, and economics* can engage with phenomena like migration* and globalization (that is, the increasing economic, political, corporate, and social ties across continental borders) through the lens of childhood history. In addition, *Centuries of Childhood* has, along with the work of the influential French historian Lucien Febvre,* led to further work in the history of emotions, which studies how feelings and the expression of feelings is learned (and therefore changes over time).[4]

The US anthropologist Sharon Stephens's* treatment of modern childhood is a prime example of such scholarship.[5] Similar examples of investigating childhood in order to understand key concepts are found in the field of philosophy.[6] The international relations scholar Alison Watson,* in arguing for the importance of childhood studies for the discipline of international relations, notes the many academic journals and conferences devoted to the study of childhood such as *Childhood: A Global Journal of Child Research; The International Journal of Children's Rights;* and the *Research Committee of Sociology of Childhood.*[7]

Summary

Centuries of Childhood is essential reading because it provokes and inspires thought about the relationship we have with the world, the way we think about it, and the consequences for our lives and for the future. It also offers a reconsideration of a central development in European history, providing insights to which scholars around the globe will continue to add.

The importance of *Centuries of Childhood* is derived from its power as a "think-piece" (meaning an opinionated analysis). It presents an example of the history of "mentalities" (or changing mind-sets) with literary merit, but also shows that human ideas are influenced by social, economic, emotional, political, religious, biological, and geographical factors.

Its ongoing appeal comes from both its thought-provoking insights and its radical conclusions. Even if these conclusions are no longer widely accepted, Ariès's work will remain important because he was the first major scholar in what is now the thriving academic discipline of childhood studies. The study of childhood will continue to teach us about the world today. Perhaps, as the English poet William Wordsworth* once wrote, "The child is father of the man."

NOTES

1   Colin A. Heywood, *History of Childhood: Children and Childhood in the West from Medieval to Modern Times* (Cambridge: Polity Press, 2001), 15.

2   Colin A. Heywood, "Centuries of Childhood: An Anniversary—and an Epitaph?" *Journal of the History of Childhood and Youth* 3, no. 3 (2010): 452.

3   Paula S. Fass, "The World is at Our Door: Why Historians of Children and Childhood Should Open up," *Journal of the History of Childhood and Youth* 1, no. 1 (Winter 2008): 11–31.

4   Roy Kozlovsky, "Architecture, Emotions and the History of Childhood," in *Childhood, Youth and Emotions in Modern History: National, Colonial and Global Perspectives*, ed. Stephanie Olsen (Basingstoke: Palgrave Macmillan, 2015), 95–118.

5   Sharon Stephens, ed., *Children and the Politics of Culture* (Princeton: Princeton University Press, 1995).

6   Michael A. Peters and Viktor Johansson, "Historicizing Subjectivity in Childhood Studies," *Linguistic and Philosophical Investigations* 11 (2012): 42–61.

7   Alison M. S. Watson, "Children and International Relations: A New Site of Knowledge?" *Review of International Studies* 32, no. 2 (2006): 239.

GLOSSARY

GLOSSARY OF TERMS

Action Française: a far-right French political movement founded in 1899. The movement became monarchist, strongly against the legacy of the French Revolution, nationalist, anti-parliamentary, and Roman Catholic.

Agrégation: a competitive French civil-service examination, which must be completed to obtain an elite teaching position in certain disciplines.

L'Ancien régime: the period in French history from the 1500s to the French Revolution in 1789 when France was ruled by a monarchy, and the social, legal, and economic structures of French life were shaped by kings and queens, and laws and the government by aristocrats.

***Annales* school:** a group of French historians who came together after 1929 and focused on social and economic history, rather than political or diplomatic history. Cofounded by Lucien Febvre and Marc Bloch, and later led by Fernand Braudel and others.

Anthropology: the study of human beings, commonly focusing on culture, society, and belief.

Art history: the term for any attempt to study paintings, sculptures, and other works of art for their historical significance and for their part in the development of art around the world throughout history.

Biology: the scientific study of living organisms, in particular, but not limited to, their cell structure, evolution, breeding, and life-spans.

Childhood studies: a recent discipline drawing on fields such as psychology (the study of the human mind and behavior), history, sociology (the study of social behavior and society), anthropology (the study of human culture and society as expressed by human behavior), and medical science.

Cognitive: anything relating to the acquisition of knowledge by the brain through thought, experience, and the senses.

Colonies: states or regions dependent on the control of a foreign power. In French history, France's notable colonies have included French Indochina, Middle Eastern states including Lebanon, and African states.

Conservative: political views emphasizing the need to preserve and uphold social traditions and norms, and promoting individual freedom and economic independence from the state.

Cultural history: the study by historians of how past people represent their cultures and how this changes over time.

Cultural studies: an intellectual school that first emerged in Britain during the 1960s and then spread internationally. Cultural studies propose an anthropological reading of social relations, examining culture as a form of lived experience.

Deconstructionism: a philosophical and literary movement that involves taking apart texts to examine the meaning of individual words, and particularly their relationship with other words; the approach is commonly applied to culture more generally. Deconstructionism assumes that words do not derive meaning from the world to which they refer, but rather from their interplay with other words.

Demography: the statistical study of any population, whether human or animal.

Early modern period: the period of European history beginning in around 1500 and ending with the French Revolution in 1789.

École des Hautes Études en Sciences Sociales: an independent division of the University of Paris founded in 1947 that specializes in humanities and social science studies. The name means School for Advanced Social Science Studies.

Economics: the branch of social services that studies the supply of and demand for goods and services, and its growth and development, and models competing ways to organize the local, national, and global economy.

Enlightenment: a movement in late seventeenth- and eighteenth-century Europe that emphasized the use of reason to increase knowledge and improve society; abuses of the Church and government were to be replaced by a free, progressive, rational, and tolerant society held together by its members' sense of their individual duty to each other to preserve enlightened sociability.

Ethnography: the study of the culture and organization of social groups by an individual who integrates themselves into the culture they study.

Eurocentrism: a world view that emphasizes the alleged superiority of European ways of life and thought to the exclusion of non-European alternatives.

Feminism: political, cultural, and intellectual views concerned with equal social, political, cultural, and economic rights for women, including equal rights in the home, workplace, within education, and in government.

French Revolution: the events of the years 1789–99 during which the French monarchy was overthrown and replaced by a republic. The French Revolution had political consequences throughout Europe.

Gender: the sum of attributes considered to represent identities such as "male" or "female."

Humanities: disciplines concerned with human life considered in nonscientific terms such as philosophy, literature, history, geography, musicology, international relations, and psychology.

Infanticide: the intentional killing of a child, usually less than 12 months old, by a parent.

Late Middle Ages: the period of European history spanning the fourteenth to the fifteenth centuries, approximately 1301–1500.

Martinique: a small island in the Caribbean Sea. Formerly a French colony, the island was transformed into an overseas department of France in 1946 and remains part of the French Republic today.

Medieval: another term for the Middle Ages; the period of European history beginning with the end of the Roman Empire in the fifth century until the fifteenth century with the foundation of modern states and the Renaissance.

Mentality: unconscious ways of thinking or mind-sets by which people view the world around them.

Middle Ages: also known as the medieval period; the period of European history spanning from the end of the Roman Empire in the fifth century until the fifteenth century.

Migration: the movement of people across regional, national, and international borders.

Nazism: the collection of beliefs, including racial superiority and the expansion of the German state, expressed by the political movement of the same name, which informed the German government led by Adolf Hitler from 1933 until 1945.

Neurobiology: a subdiscipline of neuroscience and biology that studies the operation of the brain and nervous system to understand its basic structures and how it functions.

Nuclear family: typically, two married adults together with their children, widely considered as a modern social norm. This idea is at the heart of the contemporary notion of family that *Centuries of Childhood* challenged.

Physiology: the subfield of biology focusing on the study of organisms, including the human body, its characteristics, and function.

Postcolonial studies: a subfield of the liberal arts examining the effects of global colonialism that continues to shape the contemporary world for colonizer and colonized.

Psychoanalysis: a method of analyzing thought processes and dreams that traces their origin to a person's subconscious and understands them as an expression of accumulated experience, from childhood on.

Psychology: the study of the human mind and human behavior with a view to establishing general principles through the study of individuals and groups.

Public sphere: a modern term describing the space in which members of society gather to discuss its problems and developments in public.

Reactionary: any view or school of thought that strongly opposes the current political state of affairs in favor of a return to a previous state of affairs. In Ariès's case, he was critical of modernity in favor of a return to the social customs and values of medieval royalist France.

Renaissance: the period from the end of the fourteenth to the beginning of the seventeenth centuries when European culture was reinvigorated by a focus on classical thought and forms.

Republican: a supporter of the political ideology of republicanism, according to which power should be held in the hands of the people rather than by a monarch. In France, specifically, the term designates an individual supporting the French Republic instituted in 1815. Republican scholars focus on matters concering republican France.

Roman Catholic: the largest branch of the Christian religion. The head of the Roman Catholic Church is the Pope.

Royalist: a supporter of a monarchy; in France, the term specifically applies to a supporter of the restoration of the French (Bourbon) monarchy after its overthrow during the French Revolution.

Social history: an approach to the writing of history in which the experience of everyday people, rather than the actions of monarchs or statesmen, for example, is central. The approach is associated with the Annales school of historians.

Sociology: the study of human society, particularly its organization, development over time, and social institutions and networks.

Thesis: in the field of logic, the collection of ideas that an author or thinker argues for by citing evidence and building an argument. Ariès's thesis is that childhood was invented in the Middle Ages.

Third Republic: the period of French government from 1870 until 1940—the point when France was overrun by Nazi Germany, leading to military occupation of the north of the nation, and a government of exile, Vichy France, in the south.

Vichy France: the name given to the government of Marshal Philippe Pétain from July 1940 to August 1944, which cooperated with the Nazis during World War II.

World War I: armed conflict lasting from 1914 until 1918 between the Central Powers of Austria-Hungary, Germany, and Italy, and the Allied Powers of the British Empire, France, the Russian Empire, and the United States.

World War II: the worldwide armed conflict lasting from 1939 to 1945, beginning with the German invasion of Poland. The United States later entered the war when Germany's allies, the Japanese, attacked a US naval base

PEOPLE MENTIONED IN THE TEXT

Lester Alston is an American psychologist whose work covers all aspects of childhood and child development.

Doris Desclais Berkvam (b. 1942) is a French-born literary scholar who is professor emeritus of French at Reed College, Portland, Oregon and a specialist in medieval French literature and society.

Marc Bloch (1886–1944) was a French historian of medieval France. The author of famous history books such as *La Société Féodale* (*Feudal Society*) (1939–40), he was a cofounder of the *Annales* school along with the historian Lucien Febvre.

Fernand Braudel (1902–85) was a French historian of early modern Europe, the Mediterranean, and North Africa. He is best known for his work *La Méditerranée et le monde méditerranéen à l'époque de Philippe II* (*The Mediterranean and the Mediterranean World in the Age of Philip II*) (1949).

André Burgière (b. 1938) is a French historian of family and population history in the modern period; he is interested in the history of historical writing.

Louis Chevalier (1911–2001) was a French historian and demographer whose work focused on the development and population changes of Paris in the nineteenth century.

Hugh Cunningham is a British social historian who specializes in childhood studies; he is professor emeritus of social history at the University of Kent.

Lloyd deMause (b. 1931) is an American social thinker whose major academic contributions have been to psychohistory: the study of psychological motivations of historical events.

Jacques Droz (1909–98) was a French historian of modern France and international history, including diplomatic history. He is celebrated for his work on the history of Germany and Austria, and the history of social democratic thought.

Georges Duby (1919–96) was a French historian who had a particular interest in the social and economic history of the Middle Ages, both in France and in Europe.

Émile Durkheim (1858–1917) was a French sociologist and social psychologist, widely regarded as founding the modern discipline of sociology. Among his best-known works is *Les Règles de la méthode sociologique* (*The Rules of the Sociological Method*) (1895).

Paula S. Fass is an American social and cultural historian specializing in childhood history, and professor emerita of history at the University of California at Berkeley.

Lucien Febvre (1878–1956) was a French historian of early modern Europe and founder, with Marc Bloch, of the *Annales* school. He is celebrated for works such as *The Problem of Unbelief in the Sixteenth Century: The Religion of Rabelais* (1942).

Shulamith Firestone (1945–2012) was a Canadian-born feminist whose book *The Dialectic of Sex* (1970) is internationally important for its contribution to radical feminism.

Michel Foucault (1926–84) was a French philosopher and historian best known for his theory concerning the structure of power that defines society, especially the relationship between power and knowledge.

Sigmund Freud (1856–1939) was an Austrian neurologist and founder of the theoretical and therapeutic method of psychoanalysis. Freud's theories emphasize the role of unconscious thought in human behavior.

Jacques Le Goff (1924–2014) was a French historian whose work focused on the Middle Ages. He was part of the *Annales* school, and is best known for his economic histories of trade and commerce and his religious histories of saints and religious beliefs.

Daniel Halévy (1872–1962) was a French historian and essayist whose works mounted a sustained attack on modern republican France. Halévy expressed particular interest in France under the French monarchy prior to 1789, but his work focused on the Third Republic.

Barbara A. Hanawalt (b. 1941) is an American medieval historian with a special focus on English medieval history. She is an emeritus professor of Ohio State University.

Janet Hart is an American anthropologist and professor emerita of anthropology at the University of Michigan in Ann Arbor.

Colin A. Heywood is a British historian of French history, particularly of the nineteenth century and of childhood. He is emeritus professor of modern French history at the University of Nottingham.

Patrick H. Hutton is an American historian of European intellectual history and professor emeritus of history at the University of Vermont.

Margaret L. King is professor emerita of history at Brooklyn College, including childhood history from antiquity to the present.

Emmanuel Le Roy Ladurie (b. 1929) is a French historian of France during the early modern period, with a particular interest in the French peasantry of that era. Among his best-known works is *Les Paysans de Languedoc* (*The Peasants of Languedoc*) (1966).

Claude Lévi-Strauss (1908–2009) was a French anthropologist whose most famous work is *Anthropologie structurale* (*Structural Anthropology*) (1958). Lévi-Strauss showed how human facts were limited by the logical structures of the mind.

Lucien Lévy-Bruhl (1857–1939) was a French philosopher who worked in the fields of sociology, anthropology, and ethnology. He is best known for his studies of "primitive" peoples, *Les Fonctions Mentales dans les sociétés inférieures* (*How Natives Think*) (1910).

Ferdinand Lot (1866–1952) was a French historian of medieval Europe whose work focused on the transition from the classical to the medieval period.

Robert Mandrou (1921–84) was a French historian of early modern France and a member of the *Annales* school. His major works include *Introduction à la France moderne: Essai de psychologie historique 1500–1640* (*Introduction to Modern France: An Essay in Historical Psychology 1500–1640*) (1961).

Charles Maurras (1868–1952) was a leading thinker of the right-wing organization Action Française. An influential monarchist, counterrevolutionary, and anti-parliamentarian of the early-twentieth century, his political thought anticipated some of the ideas of fascism.

Molière (Jean-Baptiste Poquelin, 1622–73) was a French playwright and actor. His work is internationally famous for its mastery of comedy.

Michel de Montaigne (1533–92) was a French philosopher of the period of European cultural history known as the Renaissance; his writing often focuses on child psychology.

Nicholas Orme is a British historian of medieval and Tudor England. He is emeritus professor of history at the University of Exeter.

Linda A. Pollock is professor of history at Tulane University, New Orleans, specializing in childhood and family history.

Laurel Reed is an American art historian who is currently assistant professor of liberal arts at the Pacific Northwest College of Arts, and a specialist in early modern cultural and visual patrimony.

Sharon Stephens (1952–98) was an American anthropologist who worked mainly at the University of Michigan, where she also combined her studies in social work and childcare.

Lawrence Stone (1919–99) was an English historian whose work focused on early modern English social history, family history, and the evolution of the English nobility.

Titian (1490–1576) was an Italian painter of the sixteenth century.

Alison M. S. Watson is head of the School of International Relations at the University of St Andrews, Scotland. Her primary research focuses on examining the place of children in the international system.

Adrian Wilson is a British historian of medicine and a senior lecturer in the history of medicine at the University of Leeds.

William Wordsworth (1770–1850) was an English poet whose poetry focused on the characteristics of childhood, among other aspects of the human condition.

WORKS CITED

WORKS CITED

Alston, Lester. "Children as Chattel." In *Small Worlds: Children and Adolescents in America, 1850–1950*, edited by Elliott West and Paula Petrik, 208–31. Lawrence: University Press of Kansas, 1992.

Ariès, Philippe. *Centuries of Childhood: A Social History of Family Life.* Translated by Robert Baldick. New York: Knopf, 1962.

— *Centuries of Childhood: A Social History of Family Life.* Translated by Robert Baldick. New York: Vintage Books, 1962.

— *Centuries of Childhood: A Social History of Family Life.* Translated by Robert Baldick. London: Pimlico, 1996.

— *Histoire des populations françaises* (*History of the French Population*). Paris: Éditions Self, 1948.

— *L'Homme devant la mort* (*The Hour of Our Death*). Paris: Le Seuil, 1977.

— *Le Temps de l'histoire* (*The Times of History*). Monaco: Éditions du Rocher, 1954.

— "The Sentimental Revolution." *Wilson Quarterly* (Autumn 1982): 46–53.

Ariès, Philippe, and Michel Winock. "L'Enfant à travers les siècles" (The Child through the Centuries). *L'Histoire* 19 (January 1980): 85–7.

Behnke Kinney, Anne, ed. *Chinese Views of Childhood.* Honolulu: University of Hawaii Press, 1995.

Braudel, Fernand. "Histoire et sciences sociales: La longue durée" (History and social science: The long duration). *Annales. Économies, Sociétés, Civilisations* 13, no. 4 (1958): 725–53.

Burgière, André. *The Annales School: An Intellectual History.* Translated by Jane Marie Todd. Ithaca, NY: Cornell University Press, 2009.

Conklin, Alice L. *A Mission to Civilize: The Republican Idea of Empire in France and West Africa, 1895–1935.* Redwood City, CA: Stanford University Press, 1997.

Corsaro, William A. *The Sociology of Childhood.* London: Sage Publications, 2005.

Cunningham, Hugh. "Histories of Childhood." *American Historical Review* 103, no. 4 (1998): 1195–208.

deMause, Lloyd, ed. *The History of Childhood.* New York: Psychohistory Press, 1974.

Desclais Berkvam, Doris. "Nature and Norreture: A Notion of Medieval Childhood and Education." *Mediaevalia* 9 (1983): 165–80.

Dosse, François. "Ariès, Philippe (Blois, 1914–Toulouse, 1984)." In *Dictionnaire des historiens français et francophones: De Grégoire de Tours à Georges Duby*, edited by Christian Amalvi, 4–6. Paris: La Boutique de l'Histoire, 2004.

Fass, Paula S. "The World is at Our Door: Why Historians of Children and Childhood Should Open up." *Journal of the History of Childhood and Youth* 1, no. 1 (2008): 11–31.

Febvre, Lucien. "Vers une autre histoire" (Towards Another History). *Revue de Métaphysique et de Morale* 63 (1949): 225–47.

Foucault, Michel. *Discipline and Punish: The Birth of the Prison*. Translated by Alan Sheridan. New York: Pantheon Books, 1977.

Google Scholar. Accessed March 14, 2016. https://scholar.google.com/scholar?hl=en&q=%22Centuries+of+Childhood%22+&btnG=&as_sdt=1%2C31.

Hanawalt, Barbara A. *Growing up in Medieval London: The Experience of Childhood in History*. Oxford: Oxford University Press, 1993.

Hart, Janet. "Reading the Radical Subject: Gramsci, Glinos, and Paralanguages of the Modern Nation." In *Intellectuals and the Articulation of the Nation*, edited by Ronald Grigor Suny and Michael Kennedy, 171–204. Ann Arbor: University of Michigan Press, 2001.

Heywood, Colin A. *A History of Childhood: Children and Childhood in the West from Medieval to Modern Times*. Cambridge: Polity Press, 2001.

— "Centuries of Childhood: An Anniversary—and an Epitaph?" *Journal of the History of Childhood and Youth* 3, no. 3 (2010): 341–65.

Hutton, Patrick H. "Late-Life Historical Reflections of Philippe Ariès on the Family in Contemporary Culture." *Journal of Family History* 26, no. 3 (July 2001): 395–410. doi: 10.1177/036319900102600305.

— "Philippe Ariès (1914–1984)." In *French Historians 1900–2000: New Historical Writing in Twentieth-Century France*, edited by Philip Daileader and Philip Whalen, 11–22. Chichester: Wiley-Blackwell, 2010.

— *Philippe Ariès and the Politics of French Cultural History*. Amherst: University of Massachusetts Press, 2004.

Kedward, Rod. *La Vie en Bleu: France and the French since 1900*. London: Allen Lane, 2005.

Keylor. William R. *Academy and Community: The Foundation of the French Historical Profession*. Cambridge, MA: Harvard University Press, 1975.

King, Margaret L. "Concepts of Childhood: What We Know and Where We Might Go." *Renaissance Quarterly* 60, no. 2 (Summer 2007): 371–407.

Kozlovsky, Roy. "Architecture, Emotions and the History of Childhood." In *Childhood, Youth and Emotions in Modern History: National, Colonial and Global Perspectives*. Edited by Stephanie Olsen, 95–118. Basingstoke: Palgrave Macmillan, 2015.

Krausman Ben-Amos, Ilana. "Adolescence as a Cultural Invention: Philippe Ariès and the Sociology of Youth." *History of the Human Sciences* 8, no. 2 (May 1995): 69–89. doi: 10.1177/095269519500800204.

Lowe, Roy. "Childhood through the Ages." In *An Introduction to Early Childhood Studies*, edited by Trisha Maynard and Nigel Thomas, 21–32. London: Sage Publications, 2004.

Mandrou, Robert. *Introduction à la France moderne: Essai de psychologie historique 1500–1640* (*Introduction to Modern France: An Essay in Historical Psychology 1500–1640*). Paris: Albin Michel, 1961.

Metcalf, Stephen. "Farewell to Mini-Me: The Fight over When Childhood Began." *Slate* (March 2002). Accessed February 14, 2014. http://www.slate.com/articles/arts/culturebox/2002/03/farewell_to_minime.html.

Miller, Naomi, and Naomi Yavneh, eds. *Gender and Early Modern Constructions of Childhood*. Farnham: Ashgate, 2011.

Morrison, Heidi. *The Global History of Childhood Reader*. London: Routledge, 2012.

Orme, Nicholas. *Medieval Children*. New Haven: Yale University Press, 2001.

Peters, Michael A., and Viktor Johansson. "Historicizing Subjectivity in Childhood Studies." *Linguistic and Philosophical Investigations* 11 (2012): 42–61.

Phillips, Adam. "Introduction." In *Centuries of Childhood* by Philippe Ariès, translated by Robert Baldick. London: Pimlico, 1996.

Pollock, Linda A. *Forgotten Children: Parent–Child Relations from 1500 to 1900*. Cambridge: Cambridge University Press, 1983.

Quenzler Brown, Irene. Review of *Centuries of Childhood*. *History of Education Quarterly* 7, no. 4 (1967): 357–68.

Qvortrup, Jens, ed. *Childhood Matters: Social Theory, Practice and Politics*. Aldershot: Avebury, 1994.

Reed, Laurel. "Art, Life, Charm and Titian's *Portrait of Clarissa Strozzi*." In *Childhood in the Middle Ages and the Renaissance: The Results of a Paradigm Shift in the History of Mentality*, edited by Albrecht Classen, 355–71. Berlin: Walter de Gruyter, 2005.

Rosenthal, Joel T., ed. *Essays on Medieval Childhood: Responses to Recent Debates*. Donington: Shaun Tyas, 2007.

Stearns, Peter N. *Childhood in World History*. New York: Routledge, 2006.

Stephens, Sharon, ed. *Children and the Politics of Culture*. Princeton: Princeton University Press, 1995.

Stone, Lawrence. *The Family, Sex, and Marriage in England 1500–1800*. London: Weidenfeld & Nicolson, 1977.

— "The Massacre of the Innocents." *New York Review of Books* (November 1974): 25–31.

Tendler, Joseph. "Jacques Droz (1909–1998)." In *French Historians 1900– 2000: New Historical Writing in Twentieth Century France*, edited by Philip Daileader and Philip Whalen, 164–79. Oxford: Blackwell, 2010.

— *Opponents of the Annales School*. Basingstoke: Palgrave Macmillan, 2013.

Watson, Alison M. S. "Children and International Relations: A New Site of Knowledge?" *Review of International Studies* 32, no. 2 (April 2006): 237–50.

Wilson, Adrian. "The Infancy of the History of Childhood: An Appraisal of Philippe Ariès." *History and Theory* 19, no. 2 (1980): 132–53.

Wilson Quarterly. "Philippe Ariès: Mentality as History." *Wilson Quarterly* 5, no. 1 (Winter 1981): 102–4. http://www.jstor.org/stable/40256047.

THE MACAT LIBRARY
BY DISCIPLINE

AFRICANA STUDIES

Chinua Achebe's *An Image of Africa: Racism in Conrad's Heart of Darkness*
W. E. B. Du Bois's *The Souls of Black Folk*
Zora Neale Huston's *Characteristics of Negro Expression*
Martin Luther King Jr's *Why We Can't Wait*
Toni Morrison's *Playing in the Dark: Whiteness in the American Literary Imagination*

ANTHROPOLOGY

Arjun Appadurai's *Modernity at Large: Cultural Dimensions of Globalisation*
Philippe Ariès's *Centuries of Childhood*
Franz Boas's *Race, Language and Culture*
Kim Chan & Renée Mauborgne's *Blue Ocean Strategy*
Jared Diamond's *Guns, Germs & Steel: the Fate of Human Societies*
Jared Diamond's *Collapse: How Societies Choose to Fail or Survive*
E. E. Evans-Pritchard's *Witchcraft, Oracles and Magic Among the Azande*
James Ferguson's *The Anti-Politics Machine*
Clifford Geertz's *The Interpretation of Cultures*
David Graeber's *Debt: the First 5000 Years*
Karen Ho's *Liquidated: An Ethnography of Wall Street*
Geert Hofstede's *Culture's Consequences: Comparing Values, Behaviors, Institutes and Organizations across Nations*
Claude Lévi-Strauss's *Structural Anthropology*
Jay Macleod's *Ain't No Makin' It: Aspirations and Attainment in a Low-Income Neighborhood*
Saba Mahmood's *The Politics of Piety: The Islamic Revival and the Feminist Subject*
Marcel Mauss's *The Gift*

BUSINESS

Jean Lave & Etienne Wenger's *Situated Learning*
Theodore Levitt's *Marketing Myopia*
Burton G. Malkiel's *A Random Walk Down Wall Street*
Douglas McGregor's *The Human Side of Enterprise*
Michael Porter's *Competitive Strategy: Creating and Sustaining Superior Performance*
John Kotter's *Leading Change*
C. K. Prahalad & Gary Hamel's *The Core Competence of the Corporation*

CRIMINOLOGY

Michelle Alexander's *The New Jim Crow: Mass Incarceration in the Age of Colorblindness*
Michael R. Gottfredson & Travis Hirschi's *A General Theory of Crime*
Richard Herrnstein & Charles A. Murray's *The Bell Curve: Intelligence and Class Structure in American Life*
Elizabeth Loftus's *Eyewitness Testimony*
Jay Macleod's *Ain't No Makin' It: Aspirations and Attainment in a Low-Income Neighborhood*
Philip Zimbardo's *The Lucifer Effect*

ECONOMICS

Janet Abu-Lughod's *Before European Hegemony*
Ha-Joon Chang's *Kicking Away the Ladder*
David Brion Davis's *The Problem of Slavery in the Age of Revolution*
Milton Friedman's *The Role of Monetary Policy*
Milton Friedman's *Capitalism and Freedom*
David Graeber's *Debt: the First 5000 Years*
Friedrich Hayek's *The Road to Serfdom*
Karen Ho's *Liquidated: An Ethnography of Wall Street*

John Maynard Keynes's *The General Theory of Employment, Interest and Money*
Charles P. Kindleberger's *Manias, Panics and Crashes*
Robert Lucas's *Why Doesn't Capital Flow from Rich to Poor Countries?*
Burton G. Malkiel's *A Random Walk Down Wall Street*
Thomas Robert Malthus's *An Essay on the Principle of Population*
Karl Marx's *Capital*
Thomas Piketty's *Capital in the Twenty-First Century*
Amartya Sen's *Development as Freedom*
Adam Smith's *The Wealth of Nations*
Nassim Nicholas Taleb's *The Black Swan: The Impact of the Highly Improbable*
Amos Tversky's & Daniel Kahneman's *Judgment under Uncertainty: Heuristics and Biases*
Mahbub Ul Haq's *Reflections on Human Development*
Max Weber's *The Protestant Ethic and the Spirit of Capitalism*

FEMINISM AND GENDER STUDIES

Judith Butler's *Gender Trouble*
Simone De Beauvoir's *The Second Sex*
Michel Foucault's *History of Sexuality*
Betty Friedan's *The Feminine Mystique*
Saba Mahmood's *The Politics of Piety: The Islamic Revival and the Feminist Subject*
Joan Wallach Scott's *Gender and the Politics of History*
Mary Wollstonecraft's *A Vindication of the Rights of Woman*
Virginia Woolf's *A Room of One's Own*

GEOGRAPHY

The Brundtland Report's *Our Common Future*
Rachel Carson's *Silent Spring*
Charles Darwin's *On the Origin of Species*
James Ferguson's *The Anti-Politics Machine*
Jane Jacobs's *The Death and Life of Great American Cities*
James Lovelock's *Gaia: A New Look at Life on Earth*
Amartya Sen's *Development as Freedom*
Mathis Wackernagel & William Rees's *Our Ecological Footprint*

HISTORY

Janet Abu-Lughod's *Before European Hegemony*
Benedict Anderson's *Imagined Communities*
Bernard Bailyn's *The Ideological Origins of the American Revolution*
Hanna Batatu's *The Old Social Classes And The Revolutionary Movements Of Iraq*
Christopher Browning's *Ordinary Men: Reserve Police Batallion 101 and the Final Solution in Poland*
Edmund Burke's *Reflections on the Revolution in France*
William Cronon's *Nature's Metropolis: Chicago And The Great West*
Alfred W. Crosby's *The Columbian Exchange*
Hamid Dabashi's *Iran: A People Interrupted*
David Brion Davis's *The Problem of Slavery in the Age of Revolution*
Nathalie Zemon Davis's *The Return of Martin Guerre*
Jared Diamond's *Guns, Germs & Steel: the Fate of Human Societies*
Frank Dikotter's *Mao's Great Famine*
John W Dower's *War Without Mercy: Race And Power In The Pacific War*
W. E. B. Du Bois's *The Souls of Black Folk*
Richard J. Evans's *In Defence of History*
Lucien Febvre's *The Problem of Unbelief in the 16th Century*
Sheila Fitzpatrick's *Everyday Stalinism*

Eric Foner's *Reconstruction: America's Unfinished Revolution, 1863-1877*
Michel Foucault's *Discipline and Punish*
Michel Foucault's *History of Sexuality*
Francis Fukuyama's *The End of History and the Last Man*
John Lewis Gaddis's *We Now Know: Rethinking Cold War History*
Ernest Gellner's *Nations and Nationalism*
Eugene Genovese's *Roll, Jordan, Roll: The World the Slaves Made*
Carlo Ginzburg's *The Night Battles*
Daniel Goldhagen's *Hitler's Willing Executioners*
Jack Goldstone's *Revolution and Rebellion in the Early Modern World*
Antonio Gramsci's *The Prison Notebooks*
Alexander Hamilton, John Jay & James Madison's *The Federalist Papers*
Christopher Hill's *The World Turned Upside Down*
Carole Hillenbrand's *The Crusades: Islamic Perspectives*
Thomas Hobbes's *Leviathan*
Eric Hobsbawm's *The Age Of Revolution*
John A. Hobson's *Imperialism: A Study*
Albert Hourani's *History of the Arab Peoples*
Samuel P. Huntington's *The Clash of Civilizations and the Remaking of World Order*
C. L. R. James's *The Black Jacobins*
Tony Judt's *Postwar: A History of Europe Since 1945*
Ernst Kantorowicz's *The King's Two Bodies: A Study in Medieval Political Theology*
Paul Kennedy's *The Rise and Fall of the Great Powers*
Ian Kershaw's *The "Hitler Myth": Image and Reality in the Third Reich*
John Maynard Keynes's *The General Theory of Employment, Interest and Money*
Charles P. Kindleberger's *Manias, Panics and Crashes*
Martin Luther King Jr's *Why We Can't Wait*
Henry Kissinger's *World Order: Reflections on the Character of Nations and the Course of History*
Thomas Kuhn's *The Structure of Scientific Revolutions*
Georges Lefebvre's *The Coming of the French Revolution*
John Locke's *Two Treatises of Government*
Niccolò Machiavelli's *The Prince*
Thomas Robert Malthus's *An Essay on the Principle of Population*
Mahmood Mamdani's *Citizen and Subject: Contemporary Africa And The Legacy Of Late Colonialism*
Karl Marx's *Capital*
Stanley Milgram's *Obedience to Authority*
John Stuart Mill's *On Liberty*
Thomas Paine's *Common Sense*
Thomas Paine's *Rights of Man*
Geoffrey Parker's *Global Crisis: War, Climate Change and Catastrophe in the Seventeenth Century*
Jonathan Riley-Smith's *The First Crusade and the Idea of Crusading*
Jean-Jacques Rousseau's *The Social Contract*
Joan Wallach Scott's *Gender and the Politics of History*
Theda Skocpol's *States and Social Revolutions*
Adam Smith's *The Wealth of Nations*
Timothy Snyder's *Bloodlands: Europe Between Hitler and Stalin*
Sun Tzu's *The Art of War*
Keith Thomas's *Religion and the Decline of Magic*
Thucydides's *The History of the Peloponnesian War*
Frederick Jackson Turner's *The Significance of the Frontier in American History*
Odd Arne Westad's *The Global Cold War: Third World Interventions And The Making Of Our Times*

LITERATURE

Chinua Achebe's *An Image of Africa: Racism in Conrad's Heart of Darkness*
Roland Barthes's *Mythologies*
Homi K. Bhabha's *The Location of Culture*
Judith Butler's *Gender Trouble*
Simone De Beauvoir's *The Second Sex*
Ferdinand De Saussure's *Course in General Linguistics*
T. S. Eliot's *The Sacred Wood: Essays on Poetry and Criticism*
Zora Neale Huston's *Characteristics of Negro Expression*
Toni Morrison's *Playing in the Dark: Whiteness in the American Literary Imagination*
Edward Said's *Orientalism*
Gayatri Chakravorty Spivak's *Can the Subaltern Speak?*
Mary Wollstonecraft's *A Vindication of the Rights of Women*
Virginia Woolf's *A Room of One's Own*

PHILOSOPHY

Elizabeth Anscombe's *Modern Moral Philosophy*
Hannah Arendt's *The Human Condition*
Aristotle's *Metaphysics*
Aristotle's *Nicomachean Ethics*
Edmund Gettier's *Is Justified True Belief Knowledge?*
Georg Wilhelm Friedrich Hegel's *Phenomenology of Spirit*
David Hume's *Dialogues Concerning Natural Religion*
David Hume's *The Enquiry for Human Understanding*
Immanuel Kant's *Religion within the Boundaries of Mere Reason*
Immanuel Kant's *Critique of Pure Reason*
Søren Kierkegaard's *The Sickness Unto Death*
Søren Kierkegaard's *Fear and Trembling*
O. S. Lewis's *The Abolition of Man*
Alasdair MacIntyre's *After Virtue*
Marcus Aurelius's *Meditations*
Friedrich Nietzsche's *On the Genealogy of Morality*
Friedrich Nietzsche's *Beyond Good and Evil*
Plato's *Republic*
Plato's *Symposium*
Jean-Jacques Rousseau's *The Social Contract*
Gilbert Ryle's *The Concept of Mind*
Baruch Spinoza's *Ethics*
Sun Tzu's *The Art of War*
Ludwig Wittgenstein's *Philosophical Investigations*

POLITICS

Benedict Anderson's *Imagined Communities*
Aristotle's *Politics*
Bernard Bailyn's *The Ideological Origins of the American Revolution*
Edmund Burke's *Reflections on the Revolution in France*
John C. Calhoun's *A Disquisition on Government*
Ha-Joon Chang's *Kicking Away the Ladder*
Hamid Dabashi's *Iran: A People Interrupted*
Hamid Dabashi's *Theology of Discontent: The Ideological Foundation of the Islamic Revolution in Iran*
Robert Dahl's *Democracy and its Critics*
Robert Dahl's *Who Governs?*
David Brion Davis's *The Problem of Slavery in the Age of Revolution*

Alexis De Tocqueville's *Democracy in America*
James Ferguson's *The Anti-Politics Machine*
Frank Dikotter's *Mao's Great Famine*
Sheila Fitzpatrick's *Everyday Stalinism*
Eric Foner's *Reconstruction: America's Unfinished Revolution, 1863-1877*
Milton Friedman's *Capitalism and Freedom*
Francis Fukuyama's *The End of History and the Last Man*
John Lewis Gaddis's *We Now Know: Rethinking Cold War History*
Ernest Gellner's *Nations and Nationalism*
David Graeber's *Debt: the First 5000 Years*
Antonio Gramsci's *The Prison Notebooks*
Alexander Hamilton, John Jay & James Madison's *The Federalist Papers*
Friedrich Hayek's *The Road to Serfdom*
Christopher Hill's *The World Turned Upside Down*
Thomas Hobbes's *Leviathan*
John A. Hobson's *Imperialism: A Study*
Samuel P. Huntington's *The Clash of Civilizations and the Remaking of World Order*
Tony Judt's *Postwar: A History of Europe Since 1945*
David C. Kang's *China Rising: Peace, Power and Order in East Asia*
Paul Kennedy's *The Rise and Fall of Great Powers*
Robert Keohane's *After Hegemony*
Martin Luther King Jr.'s *Why We Can't Wait*
Henry Kissinger's *World Order: Reflections on the Character of Nations and the Course of History*
John Locke's *Two Treatises of Government*
Niccolò Machiavelli's *The Prince*
Thomas Robert Malthus's *An Essay on the Principle of Population*
Mahmood Mamdani's *Citizen and Subject: Contemporary Africa And The Legacy Of Late Colonialism*
Karl Marx's *Capital*
John Stuart Mill's *On Liberty*
John Stuart Mill's *Utilitarianism*
Hans Morgenthau's *Politics Among Nations*
Thomas Paine's *Common Sense*
Thomas Paine's *Rights of Man*
Thomas Piketty's *Capital in the Twenty-First Century*
Robert D. Putman's *Bowling Alone*
John Rawls's *Theory of Justice*
Jean-Jacques Rousseau's *The Social Contract*
Theda Skocpol's *States and Social Revolutions*
Adam Smith's *The Wealth of Nations*
Sun Tzu's *The Art of War*
Henry David Thoreau's *Civil Disobedience*
Thucydides's *The History of the Peloponnesian War*
Kenneth Waltz's *Theory of International Politics*
Max Weber's *Politics as a Vocation*
Odd Arne Westad's *The Global Cold War: Third World Interventions And The Making Of Our Times*

POSTCOLONIAL STUDIES

Roland Barthes's *Mythologies*
Frantz Fanon's *Black Skin, White Masks*
Homi K. Bhabha's *The Location of Culture*
Gustavo Gutiérrez's *A Theology of Liberation*
Edward Said's *Orientalism*
Gayatri Chakravorty Spivak's *Can the Subaltern Speak?*

PSYCHOLOGY

Gordon Allport's *The Nature of Prejudice*
Alan Baddeley & Graham Hitch's *Aggression: A Social Learning Analysis*
Albert Bandura's *Aggression: A Social Learning Analysis*
Leon Festinger's *A Theory of Cognitive Dissonance*
Sigmund Freud's *The Interpretation of Dreams*
Betty Friedan's *The Feminine Mystique*
Michael R. Gottfredson & Travis Hirschi's *A General Theory of Crime*
Eric Hoffer's *The True Believer: Thoughts on the Nature of Mass Movements*
William James's *Principles of Psychology*
Elizabeth Loftus's *Eyewitness Testimony*
A. H. Maslow's *A Theory of Human Motivation*
Stanley Milgram's *Obedience to Authority*
Steven Pinker's *The Better Angels of Our Nature*
Oliver Sacks's *The Man Who Mistook His Wife For a Hat*
Richard Thaler & Cass Sunstein's *Nudge: Improving Decisions About Health, Wealth and Happiness*
Amos Tversky's *Judgment under Uncertainty: Heuristics and Biases*
Philip Zimbardo's *The Lucifer Effect*

SCIENCE

Rachel Carson's *Silent Spring*
William Cronon's *Nature's Metropolis: Chicago And The Great West*
Alfred W. Crosby's *The Columbian Exchange*
Charles Darwin's *On the Origin of Species*
Richard Dawkins's *The Selfish Gene*
Thomas Kuhn's *The Structure of Scientific Revolutions*
Geoffrey Parker's *Global Crisis: War, Climate Change and Catastrophe in the Seventeenth Century*
Mathis Wackernagel & William Rees's *Our Ecological Footprint*

SOCIOLOGY

Michelle Alexander's *The New Jim Crow: Mass Incarceration in the Age of Colorblindness*
Gordon Allport's *The Nature of Prejudice*
Albert Bandura's *Aggression: A Social Learning Analysis*
Hanna Batatu's *The Old Social Classes And The Revolutionary Movements Of Iraq*
Ha-Joon Chang's *Kicking Away the Ladder*
W. E. B. Du Bois's *The Souls of Black Folk*
Émile Durkheim's *On Suicide*
Frantz Fanon's *Black Skin, White Masks*
Frantz Fanon's *The Wretched of the Earth*
Eric Foner's *Reconstruction: America's Unfinished Revolution, 1863-1877*
Eugene Genovese's *Roll, Jordan, Roll: The World the Slaves Made*
Jack Goldstone's *Revolution and Rebellion in the Early Modern World*
Antonio Gramsci's *The Prison Notebooks*
Richard Herrnstein & Charles A Murray's *The Bell Curve: Intelligence and Class Structure in American Life*
Eric Hoffer's *The True Believer: Thoughts on the Nature of Mass Movements*
Jane Jacobs's *The Death and Life of Great American Cities*
Robert Lucas's *Why Doesn't Capital Flow from Rich to Poor Countries?*
Jay Macleod's *Ain't No Makin' It: Aspirations and Attainment in a Low Income Neighborhood*
Elaine May's *Homeward Bound: American Families in the Cold War Era*
Douglas McGregor's *The Human Side of Enterprise*
C. Wright Mills's *The Sociological Imagination*

Thomas Piketty's *Capital in the Twenty-First Century*
Robert D. Putman's *Bowling Alone*
David Riesman's *The Lonely Crowd: A Study of the Changing American Character*
Edward Said's *Orientalism*
Joan Wallach Scott's *Gender and the Politics of History*
Theda Skocpol's *States and Social Revolutions*
Max Weber's *The Protestant Ethic and the Spirit of Capitalism*

THEOLOGY

Augustine's *Confessions*
Benedict's *Rule of St Benedict*
Gustavo Gutiérrez's *A Theology of Liberation*
Carole Hillenbrand's *The Crusades: Islamic Perspectives*
David Hume's *Dialogues Concerning Natural Religion*
Immanuel Kant's *Religion within the Boundaries of Mere Reason*
Ernst Kantorowicz's *The King's Two Bodies: A Study in Medieval Political Theology*
Søren Kierkegaard's *The Sickness Unto Death*
C. S. Lewis's *The Abolition of Man*
Saba Mahmood's *The Politics of Piety: The Islamic Revival and the Feminist Subject*
Baruch Spinoza's *Ethics*
Keith Thomas's *Religion and the Decline of Magic*

COMING SOON

Chris Argyris's *The Individual and the Organisation*
Seyla Benhabib's *The Rights of Others*
Walter Benjamin's *The Work Of Art in the Age of Mechanical Reproduction*
John Berger's *Ways of Seeing*
Pierre Bourdieu's *Outline of a Theory of Practice*
Mary Douglas's *Purity and Danger*
Roland Dworkin's *Taking Rights Seriously*
James G. March's *Exploration and Exploitation in Organisational Learning*
Ikujiro Nonaka's *A Dynamic Theory of Organizational Knowledge Creation*
Griselda Pollock's *Vision and Difference*
Amartya Sen's *Inequality Re-Examined*
Susan Sontag's *On Photography*
Yasser Tabbaa's *The Transformation of Islamic Art*
Ludwig von Mises's *Theory of Money and Credit*

Macat Disciplines

Access the greatest ideas and thinkers across entire disciplines, including

Postcolonial Studies

Roland Barthes's *Mythologies*
Frantz Fanon's *Black Skin, White Masks*
Homi K. Bhabha's *The Location of Culture*
Gustavo Gutiérrez's *A Theology of Liberation*
Edward Said's *Orientalism*
Gayatri Chakravorty Spivak's *Can the Subaltern Speak?*

Macat analyses are available from all good bookshops and libraries.

Access hundreds of analyses through one, multimedia tool.
Join free for one month **library.macat.com**

CPSIA information can be obtained
at www.ICGtesting.com
Printed in the USA
LVHW080248180320
650409LV00014B/1142

9 781912 128815